THE
AMERICAN
MARTYROLOGY

THE AMERICAN MARTYROLOGY

INCLUDING

all the SAINTS *and* BLESSEDS
of the Catholic Church *generally venerated in the*
UNITED STATES OF AMERICA

TOGETHER WITH

the VENERABLES, *the* SERVANTS OF GOD,
and others who died with the reputation of
SANCTITY *or* MARTYRDOM.

ARX PUBLISHING
MERCHANTVILLE, NEW JERSEY

IN THE YEAR OF OUR LORD
MMXV

©2015 Arx Publishing, LLC
Merchantville, NJ

NIHIL OBSTAT:
Reverend Charles P. Connor, Ph.D., *Censor Librorum*

IMPRIMATUR:
Most Reverend Joseph C. Bambera,
Bishop of the Diocese of Scranton

November 20, 2014

Printed in the United States of America

ISBN 978-1-935228-13-4

When the great American Catholic historian John Gilmary Shea published his *Pictorial Lives of the Saints* in 1889, he appended to it a "Lives of the American Saints Recently Placed in the Proper for the United States." This section, interpreting America as widely as possible, had a grand total of three saints in it: one from Mexico and two from South America.

A move was already afoot though for examples of heroic sanctity closer to home. John O'Kane Murray's 1882 book "Lives of the Catholic Heroes and Heroines of America" presented the nation with a mix of lay Catholic notables like Columbus, members of the hierarchy, and missionaries and martyrs. In 1884, the Third Plenary Council of Baltimore discussed and then petitioned Pope Leo XIII for the Causes of the North American Martyrs and Kateri Tekakwitha. Two years later the Seventh Provincial Council of Quebec submitted a similar petition on behalf of Canada.

These works stimulated the desire for a fuller catalog of national sanctity. A "Martyrologium Americanum" appeared in the *American Catholic Researches* first in 1906, and then again with revisions and corrections in 1907. A similar list appeared under the entry "Catholic Indian Missions of the United States" in volume 10 of the *Catholic Encyclopedia*, published in 1911. However, these were less martyrologies than chronological lists of priests who perished in their mission fields.

Father F. G. Holweck of St. Louis can be said to be the father of American Martyrology in the true sense. His article in the *Catholic Historical Review* for 1921 marked an important step forward from earlier endeavors. Father

Holweck included not only missionary priests but all martyrs and Servants of God, and he gave for each name a short biographical sketch in the style of the Roman Martyrology. More importantly, he abandoned the chronological approach and instead followed the order of the calendar year, listing the martyrs and confessors by dates of death when known.

Since Holweck's time there has been consistent interest in updating the list, and the American bishops have continued to put causes forward. The most ambitious effort ever came in 1941. In that year, the Commission for the Cause of Canonization of the Martyrs of the United States, headed by Bishop John Mark Gannon of Erie, forwarded to the Sacred Congregation of Rites a meticulously assembled document of 116 names. Pope Pius XII told Bishop Gannon at the time "this cause is beautiful...most beautiful", but it seems to have been indefinitely stalled by the Second World War. The causes went forward, but piecemeal. Some of those 116 names made it to the altar in subsequent years, others have had their causes opened at the diocesan level, and others still remain almost unknown to American Catholics.

In recent years there has been a flood of American saints, blesseds, and venerables to add to the missionary martyrs of colonial times. So aggressively have American Catholics sought recognition of sanctity that, at the current pace, even a decade is almost too great a delay for new editions of the martyrology.

This work is in some ways an update to Fr. Holweck's list, and in some ways an entirely new effort. The goal, of course, is the same: to provide a catalog of the saints and martyrs that have a special connection to the United States. A simple updating of Holweck's list with new American saints, blesseds, and servants of God might have sufficed, except that a list with only American-oriented feast days is rather detached from the liturgical year as actually observed in this country, and anyone using it devotionally would have had to supplement it with appropriate entries from the Roman Martyrology, which is not an ideal arrangement.

Thus, I have incorporated here all the feast days generally observed or commemorated by Latin Rite Catholics in the United States. The entries for non-American saints were largely taken from the Roman Martyrology in English published in 1916 by the John Murphy Company, Baltimore, with additions and modifications as necessary. The saints and feasts of our national calendar* were mostly condensed from Holweck's original work but some also from the Roman Martyrology. Finally, I have included days that are commonly observed in some fashion in American churches, whether through votive Masses, dedicated propers, or extra-liturgical prayers after Mass: most notably Respect Life day on January 22, Independence Day on July 4, and Thanksgiving Day on the fourth Thursday of November.

One can find numerous lists of American Saints, Blesseds, Venerables, and Servants of God on the Internet, but the

---

* Aside from those of religious communities, there are three calendars in use. These are the current General Roman calendar as modified by the U.S. Conference of Catholic Bishops, the Roman calendar used in America in 1962 as authorized by *Summorum Pontificum*, and the calendar of the Ordinariate of the Chair of St. Peter as authorized by *Anglicanorum Cœtibus*. I have simply combined the feasts of all three. Doing so allows us to partially correct some current oddities, namely that most Catholics are apt to find St. Valentine's Day remembered at the department stores and not at their local parish. Combining the calendars also gives us a very appropriate mix of Roman, English, and American saints.

criteria used in compiling them seems overly broad. For this work I have been somewhat stricter, omitting a few Servants of God whose connection with the United States was but minimal. These are Teresa Fardella di Blasi, born in New York but brought to Italy at age two; William Gagnon, born in Dover, New Hampshire but mainly a resident of Canada; Antonietta Giugliano, born in New York City but a resident of Italy since age six; Mario Hiriart, a Chilean who died while being treated for cancer in the U.S.; James Maginn, S.S.C., born in Butte, Montana but raised in Ireland; Rossella Petrellese, an Italian who died after spinal surgery in Rochester, Minnesota; Federico Salvador Ramon, resident of Spain and Mexico who died in a San Diego hospital; and Erno Tindira, born in Latrobe, Pennsylvania but active in the diocese of Mukachevo, Ukraine.

One element here that stands out from the Roman Martyrology is the presence of putative martyrs and Servants of God not sanctioned for liturgical veneration. It was done here for the same reason Holweck and others included these individuals in the past, and for the same reasons that inspired the local martyrologies of ancient times: to keep their memory alive within a Christian community and to encourage intercessory devotion to them. Some of the individuals reputed for martyrdom or sanctity may eventually be canonized, but this is by no means certain, and it is important not to assume that they will.

Public and liturgical declarations of sanctity are absolutely forbidden for those who have not been beatified or canonized, as is made clear in the Sacred Congregation of Rites's document *Norms To Be Observed In Inquiries Made By Bishops In The Causes Of Saints* (1983):

36. Any solemn celebrations or panegyric speeches about Servants of God whose sanctity of life is still being legitimately examined are prohibited in Churches. Furthermore, one must also refrain, even outside of Church, from any acts which could mislead the faithful into thinking that the inquiry conducted by the Bishop into the life of the Servant of God and his virtues or martyrdom carries with it the certitude that the Servant of God will be one day canonized.

and in the instruction *Sanctorum Mater* (2007):

Art. 117 - 1. In accordance with the dispositions of Pope Urban VIII, it is prohibited for a Servant of God to be an object of public ecclesiastical cult without the previous authorization of the Holy See .

However, the latter then goes on to state explicitly:

2. Such dispositions do not impede, in any way, private devotion toward the Servant of God and the spontaneous spreading of his reputation of holiness or martyrdom and of intercessory power.

This is exactly the spirit in which this work is offered: as a source of private devotion. It is meant to help cultivate that intercessory prayer which can bind us more closely with the Church Triumphant and, God willing, provide the impetus for additional names to be raised to the altars. Candidates for sainthood cannot be officially recognized without popular devotion, and there can be no popular devotion if the candidates are not known. To that end, it is helpful to reflect on them not only as historical subjects but also as a regular part of a yearly devotional cycle where they may someday join those commemorated in the liturgy.

For all these reasons, it is only prudent to separate those approved by the Holy See for veneration from the others, not only within the text but also in the kinds of prayers used.

Thus, each entry here is divided into two distinct categories, separated with a cross ✛. The first category in Roman type is comprised of canonized saints and blesseds of approved and longstanding veneration. It is exactly analogous to the Roman Martyrology traditionally read after the office of Prime in the Breviary, so it ends with the traditional language of the *Pretiosa*: "Precious in the Lord is the death of His saints." The second category in smaller, italic type begins "Among those with the reputation of [martyrdom/sanctity]" and ends with some language taken from Prime but chiefly based on the private prayers typically offered for the canonization of a Servant of God: "Look upon Thy servants, O Lord, and if it be Thy will, glorify them and number them among the saints."

Finally, in the spirit of the medieval necrologies, whereby monastics added the names of their deceased to their martyrologies, it is most appropriate to inscribe in these pages the names of deceased family and friends on their dates of death, and to offer prayers for their souls. An example of such a prayer has been given to complete the recitation of the martyrology.

Claudio R. Salvucci
McMichaels, Pennsylvania 2015

If it were as easy today to obtain the honor of the altars as it was a thousand years ago, the calendars of all the dioceses of the United States would show many feasts of local saints, martyrs, confessors and virgins. Since, however, the right of beatification and canonization has been reserved, first to Councils (in the 11th century), then to the Holy See exclusively (in 1634), the complicated mode of procedure has made canonizations rare occurrences in countries not belonging to the Latin races; yet the time may not be far distant when even the United States and Canada will kneel at the altars of duly canonized American Saints.

The American Martyrology which we have compiled, aims at giving the names of those Christian heroes who have died for Christ or for some Christian virtue, whilst laboring within the limits of the United States, or of those who have some special relation to them. This rule excludes the great heroes of Canada, Fathers Brebeuf, Lallemant, etc., who never set foot on United States territory.*

We have found three lists of American Martyrs: one in the *Catholic Encyclopedia* (vol. x, p. 390), another in the *American Catholic Historical Researches* (October 1906, p. 332) and a third, revised list, in the same publication (January, 1907, p. 75). These three lists simply give in chronological order the names of the martyrs and the dates and places of their martyrdom. Our present Martyrology follows the order of the Calendar and adds to the names a short sketch of the life of each martyr, as far as particulars are known. Where

---

* The Canadian martyrs are nevertheless included in the 2015 edition, as they were canonized as a group and are venerated that way in the U.S.

the date of death is unknown, we arbitrarily assigned a day, marking it with an asterisk.

We have added to the names of these martyrs those of the Venerable Servants of God whose process of beatification has, in some way, been inaugurated, e.g., Junipero Serra, Bishop Neumann, Madame Duchesne and others. The terms "martyr," "confessor" and "virgin" are used merely from convenience, it being understood that no official act of the Church authorizes the application of these terms to any of the missionaries or to their converts.

Our principal sources have been Shea, *Catholic Missions amongst the Indian Tribes of the United States*, New York, 1855; Id. *The Catholic Church in Colonial Days*, New York, 1886; and Campbell, *Pioneer Priests of North America*, New York, 1910. We have also freely used Hammer, *Die Franziskaner in den Ver. Staaten Nordamerikas*, Cologne, 1892. Where the source is not given after the sketch, the information is taken from Shea; in fact, both of his works were used for nearly every sketch.

—Rev. F. G. Holweck, 1921.

RUBRICS

To use this book devotionally, always begin with the date, along with any entries for movable feasts, if any. Then read the entries for saints and blesseds. Conclude with:

And in other places many other Holy Martyrs and Confessors and holy Virgins.
Response: Thanks be to God.
Verse: Precious in the sight of the Lord.
Response: is the death of His saints.

Next, or first if there are no saints or blesseds, read the entries in italics after the cross ✛, beginning with: Among those with the reputation...etc. *Conclude with the prayer:*

Look upon Thy servants, O Lord, and if it be Thy will, glorify them and number them among the saints. Amen.

Finally, on the anniversaries of their passing, deceased loved ones may be remembered with the prayer:

On the same day, the anniversary of the passing of our [father/mother/friend, *etc.*] N., who was dear to our household. Eternal rest grant unto him [or her, *etc.*] O Lord, and may the perpetual light shine upon him. May his soul and the souls of all the faithful departed rest in peace, Amen.

MOVABLE FEASTS

The movable feasts cannot be set out in the Martyrology, because they are kept on different days every year. They are put in this place, in order that after naming the day of the month, each one may be announced before reading the Martyrology of the day on which it shall occur in that year, as follows:

Saturday after the last Sunday of the liturgical year.

The First Sunday of the Advent of our Lord Jesus Christ, to whom is honor and glory forever and ever.

Saturday preceding Sunday the 3d, 4th, or 5th of January, or when Sunday does not fall on any of these dates, the first day of January. †

The feast of the most holy Name of Jesus.

Saturday before Septuagesima Sunday. †

Septuagesima Sunday, on which the canticle of the Lord, Alleluia, ceases to be said.

Tuesday after Quinquagesima Sunday.

Ash Wednesday, and the beginning of the fast of the most holy season of Lent.

Saturday before Palm Sunday.

Palm Sunday, when our Lord Jesus Christ, according to the prophecy of Zachary, entered Jerusalem, sitting upon the foal of an ass, and was met by the multitude bearing palms.

On this day which the Lord has made, is the solemnity of solemnities, and our Passover; the Resurrection of our Savior Jesus Christ according to the flesh.

Then are read the day of the month and the Martyrology of the following day.

Ascension Eve.

On Mount Olivet, the Ascension of our Lord Jesus Christ.

Pentecost Eve.

The day of Pentecost, when the Holy Ghost came upon the disciples at Jerusalem in the shape of fiery tongues.

Saturday within the octave of Pentecost.

The feast of the most holy and indivisible Trinity.

Saturday after the feast of the Most Holy Trinity.

The feast of Corpus Christi, the most sacred Body of Christ.

Thursday after Corpus Christi.

The feast of the most Sacred Heart of Jesus.

The Last Sunday in October.†

The feast of the Kingship of Our Lord Jesus Christ.

The Fourth Thursday in November.

The feast of Thanksgiving, in gratitude for the many favors of Almighty God.

Saturday before the last Sunday of the liturgical year.

The feast of Our Lord Jesus Christ, King of the Universe.

† *In churches using the traditional Missal of John XXIII.*

Circumcision

Conversion of St. Paul

Epiphany

St. Agnes

St. John Chrysostom

January

The First of January.

The Circumcision of our Lord Jesus Christ, and the octave of His Nativity, and the Solemnity of Mary, the Mother of God.

The Second of January.

The memory of Saints Basil the Great and Gregory Nazianzen, bishops and doctors of the Church, whose feast was moved to this day by Pope Paul VI. They are honored by other churches on June 14th and May 9th.

The Third of January.

The Feast of the Most Holy Name of Jesus, at some churches kept on the first Sunday of the year or on January 2nd.

St. Elizabeth Ann Seton

The Fourth of January.

A t Emmitsburg, Maryland, the memory of Saint
Elizabeth Ann Seton, widow and foundress of
the Sisters of Charity in the United States. A convert
from Anglicanism, she, after many privations, opened
a school for girls, next to the chapel of St. Mary's
Seminary, Baltimore. When postulants arrived, she
took vows privately before Archbishop Carroll and
the community was transferred to Emmitsburg.
Great spiritual desolation purified her soul during a
great portion of her religious life, but she cheerfully
took the royal road of the cross until she died of a
pulmonary affliction, on the 4th of January.

The Fifth of January.

A t Philadelphia, Pennsylvania, the memory of
Saint John Nepomucene Neumann, bishop. He
was born in Bohemia, incardinated and ordained by
Bishop Dubois and sent to western New York. After
having built St. Philomena's Church at Pittsburgh,
he was made vice-provincial of the Redemptorists
in America. Pius IX commanded him to accept the
bishopric of Philadelphia, and one of his first acts
was to provide for Catholic schools. Noted for his
devotion to the Blessed Sacrament, he was the first
American Bishop to introduce the Forty Hours'
Devotion into his diocese. He died there and was

buried in a vault before the altar in a lower chapel of St. Peter's Redemptorist Church, Philadelphia. He was enrolled in the catalog of the saints by Pope Saint John Paul II.

The Sixth of January.

The Epiphany of Our Lord.

The Seventh of January.

At Barcelona, Spain, the birthday of St. Raymond of Penyafort, of the Order of Preachers, celebrated for his sanctity and learning. His festival is kept by many churches on this day and by others on the 23rd of January.

The Tenth of January.

Among those with the reputation of sanctity, at Washington, D.C., the Servant of God Mary Virginia Merrick, foundress of the Christ Child Society.

The Twelfth of January.

At Monkwearmouth, in England, the birthday of St. Benedict Biscop, abbot and confessor.

St. John Nepomucene Neumann

The Thirteenth of January.

At Poitiers, in France, the birthday of St. Hilary, bishop and confessor of the Catholic faith, which he courageously defended, and for which he was banished four years to Phrygia, where, among other miracles, he raised a man from the dead. Pius IX declared him Doctor of the Church. His festival is kept by many on this day and by some on the 14th of this month.

The Fourteenth of January.

St. Hilary, bishop of Poitiers and confessor, who entered heaven on the thirteenth day of this month. — At Nola, in Campania, the birthday of St. Felix, priest, who after being subjected to torments by the persecutors, was cast into prison and extended, bound hand and foot, on shells and broken earthenware. In the night, however, his bonds were loosened and he was delivered by an angel. The persecution over, he brought many to the faith of Christ by his exemplary life and teaching, and, renowned for miracles, rested in peace.

The Fifteenth of January.

St. Paul, the first hermit, who was carried to the home of the blessed on the tenth of this month.

— In the diocese of Angers, St. Maurus, abbot and disciple of St. Benedict. He made great progress with so able a master, for while he was still under the Saint's instruction he miraculously walked upon water, a prodigy unheard of since the days of St. Peter. Sent later to France by St. Benedict, he built a famous monastery, which he governed for forty years, and after performing striking miracles, he rested in peace.

The Sixteenth of January.

At Rome, on the Salarian way, the birthday of the pope St. Marcellus, a martyr, for the confession of the Catholic faith. By command of the tyrant Maxentius he was first beaten with clubs, then sent to take care of animals, with a guard to watch him. In this servile office, dressed in hair cloth, he departed this life. ✝ *Among those with the reputation of sanctity, at Yauco, Puerto Rico, the Servant of God Mother Dominga Guzman Florit, O.P., foundress of the Dominican Sisters of Fatima.*

The Seventeenth of January.

In Thebais, St. Anthony, abbot and spiritual guide of many monks. He was most celebrated for his life and miracles, of which St. Athanasius has written a detailed account. His sacred body was found by divine revelation, during the reign of the emperor Justinian, and brought to Alexandria, where it was buried in the church of St. John the Baptist.

The Eighteenth of January.

At Rome, under the emperor Claudius, the passion of St. Prisca, virgin and martyr, who, after undergoing many torments, was crowned with martyrdom.

The Nineteenth of January.

At Rome, on the Cornelian road, the holy martyrs Marius and his wife Martha, with their sons Audifax and Abachum, noble Persians, who came to Rome, through devotion, in the time of the emperor Claudius. After they had been beaten with rods, tortured on the rack and with fire, lacerated with iron hooks, and had endured the cutting off of their hands, Martha was put to death in the place called Nympha. The others were beheaded and cast into the flames.— Also, St. Canute, king and martyr, whose birthday is the 7th of this month. ✝ *Among those with the reputation of holiness, at Marquette, Michigan, the memory of Venerable Frederic Irenaeus Baraga, bishop. He was born in Slovenia, was ordained, and emigrated to the United States. There he ministered to the Ottawa Indians at the mission of Arbre Croche and then at L'Anse, learning the Ottawa language*

*and publishing several works in it. He was made the first bishop
of the Diocese of Sault Sainte Marie, Michigan, now the diocese of
Marquette, where he served until his death. Pope Benedict XVI
declared his virtues heroic.*

The Twentieth of January.

A t Rome, the birthday of St. Fabian, pope, who
suffered martyrdom in the time of Decius, and
was buried in the cemetery of Callistus. — In the same
place, in the catacombs, the martyr St. Sebastian. He
was commander of the first cohort, under the emperor
Diocletian, but for professing Christianity he was
bound to a tree in the center of a vast field, shot with
arrows by the soldiers, and beaten with clubs until he
expired.

The Twenty-first of January.

A t Rome, the passion of St. Agnes, virgin, who
under Symphronius, governor of the city, was
thrown into the fire, but as it was extinguished by
her prayers, she was struck with the sword. Of her St.
Jerome writes: "Agnes is praised in the writings and by
the tongues of all nations, especially in the churches.
She overcame the weakness of her age, conquered the
cruelty of the tyrant, and consecrated her chastity by
martyrdom." + *Among those with the reputation of sanctity, at
Germantown, New York the memory of Venerable Mother Mary*

Angeline Teresa O. Cam., Foundress. She was born in Mountjoy, Northern Ireland and joined the Little Sisters of the Poor in France; she was soon sent to a nursing home operated by the order in New York. But finding that the needs of the elderly in America required a new approach, on the advice of Cardinal Hayes she and six other sisters withdrew from their former congregation and formed the Carmelite Sisters for the Aged and Infirm. Pope Benedict XVI proclaimed her virtues heroic.

The Twenty-second of January.

The national day of penance for the sin of abortion and of prayer for the unborn. If it falls upon a Sunday, this observance is postponed until the following day. — At Valencia, in Spain, while the wicked Dacian was governor, St. Vincent, deacon and martyr, who, after suffering imprisonment, hunger, torture, the disjointing of his limbs; after being burned with plates of heated metal and on the gridiron, and tormented in other ways, took his flight to heaven, there to receive the reward of martyrdom. — At Rome, at Aquæ Salviæ, St. Anastasius, a Persian monk, who, after suffering much at Cæsarea, in Palestine, from imprisonment, stripes and fetters, had to bear many afflictions from Chosroes, king of Persia, who caused him to be beheaded.

The Twenty-third of January.

At Kalaupapa, Hawai'i, the memory of St. Mother Marianne Cope, O.S.F., religious. She was born in Heppenheim, Germany and was brought to Syracuse, New York as an infant by her family. There she joined the Sisters of the Third Order Regular of St. Francis and served as a Superior General of St. Joseph's Hospital. At the request of King Kalakaua, she and six other Sisters relocated to Hawai'i to care for the lepers there. They managed Kaka'ako Branch Hospital on Oahu, established Malulani Hospital on Maui, and took over the leper colony at Molokai from Father Damien, not only caring for the sick but also their healthy but isolated children. Her birthday is on August 9. — At Barcelona, St. Raymond of Penyafort. His birthday is the 7th of January. — At Rome, the holy virgin and martyr Emerentiana. Being only a catechumen, she was stoned to death by the Gentiles, whilst praying at the tomb of St. Agnes, her foster sister.

The Twenty-fourth of January.

The birthday of St. Timothy, disciple of the apostle St. Paul, who ordained him bishop of Ephesus. After many combats for Christ, he was stoned for reprehending those who offered sacrifices to Diana, and shortly after went peacefully to his rest in the Lord. — In many places, the feast of the St. Francis de Sales, bishop, whose translation is remembered on the 29th of January.

The Twenty-fifth of January.

The conversion of St. Paul the Apostle, which happened the second year after the Ascension of Our Lord. ✝ *Among those with the reputation of martyrdom, at Patali, in the country of the Apalache Indians, Florida, the memory of the Franciscan missionaries Juan de Parga and Marcos Delgado. When during the war of Spanish succession Governor Moore of South Carolina with his Apalachicola allies invaded Florida and marched into the Apalache country to sell the Indian converts as slaves, Father Juan de Parga, the missionary of Patali, addressed the Indians, urging them to fight bravely, for God's holy law, as no death could be more glorious than to perish for the faith and truth. After the unfortunate battle of Ayubale, Father Parga, under the eyes of Moore, was burned by the Indians at the stake, beheaded and his leg cut off. Another Religious, Marcos Delgado, endeavoring to save Father Parga, was also slain. They were buried at Ybitacucho.*

The Twenty-sixth of January.

In many places, the feast of Sts. Timothy and Titus, disciples, who are elsewhere honored on January 24th and February 6th. — At Smyrna, the birthday of St. Polycarp, a disciple of the Apostle St. John, who consecrated him bishop of that city and Primate of all Asia. Afterwards, under Marcus Antoninus and Lucius Aurelius Commodus, whilst the proconsul was sitting in the judgment, and all the people in the amphitheater were clamoring against him, he was condemned to the flames. But as he received no injury from them, he was pierced with a sword, and thus received the crown of martyrdom. ✝ *Among those with the reputation of martyrdom, among the Tanos Indians of New Mexico the memory of Father Manuel Beltran, O.F.M. After the reestablishment of the missions in New Mexico, Father Manuel was sent to a church near a pueblo of Yumas and Tanos. He labored there a few years, but his own Indians rose against him and most cruelly slew him. After his death, as all other missionaries had been driven away to El Paso, the once flourishing Church of New Mexico disappeared.*

The Twenty-seventh of January.

At Constantinople, St. John, bishop, who was surnamed Chrysostom, on account of his golden flow of eloquence. He greatly promoted the interests of the Christian religion by his preaching and exemplary life, and after many toils, closed his life in banishment. His sacred body was brought to Constantinople on this day, in the reign of Theodosius the younger; it was afterwards taken to Rome and placed in the basilica of the Prince of the Apostles. This illustrious preacher of the Word of God Pius X declared and appointed heavenly patron of sacred orators. — At

Brescia, Italy, the birthday of St. Angela Merici, virgin, foundress of the Order of Nuns of St. Ursula, whose principal aim is to direct young girls in the ways of the Lord. She is honored by many on this day, and by some on the first of June.

The Twenty-eighth of January

At Barcelona, in Spain, St. Peter Nolasco, confessor, and founder of the order of Mercedarians, renowned for virtue and miracles, who slept in the Lord on the 25th of December. — In many places, the feast of St. Thomas Aquinas, priest and doctor. His memorial is kept by others on the 7th of March. — At Rome, the second feast of St. Agnes.

The Twenty-ninth of January.

At Lyons, in France, St. Francis de Sales, bishop of Geneva, ranked among the saints by Alexander VII, because of his ardent zeal for the conversion of heretics, and declared a Doctor of the universal Church. His relics were translated on this day from Lyons to Annecy; his birthday is on the 28th of December. In some places, he is remembered on this day, but in many places he is honored on the 24th of this month.

The Thirtieth of January.

At Rome, St. Martina, virgin, who endured various kinds of torments, and being beheaded, received the palm of martyrdom.

The Thirty-first of January.

At Turin, the birthday of St. John Bosco, confessor, founder of the Salesian Congregation and of the Institute of the Daughters of Mary, Help of Christians. Conspicuous for his zeal for souls and for the propagation of the faith, he was canonized in 1934 by Pope Pius XI. ✝ *Among those with the reputation of martyrdom, near Tallahassee, Florida, the memory of Father Angel Miranda, O.F.M., the lieutenant Juan Ruiz Mejia, the Indians Antonio Enija, Amador Cuipa Feliciano and companions. When Governor Moore of South Carolina attacked the Spanish missions in the Apalache country, after the battle of Ayubale, P. Miranda and Lieutenant Mejia with many Indian converts fell into the hands of Moore and his Indian allies. Since the Spanish officer could not furnish the ransom demanded, Father Miranda, Mejia, some soldiers and a number of Christian Indians from the town of St. Luis, were burnt at the stake. Some of the Indians, while undergoing the torture showed in prayer and exhortation the heroism of Christian martyrs.*

St. Agatha

Chair of St. Peter

Presentation

St. Valentine

Ash Wednesday

February

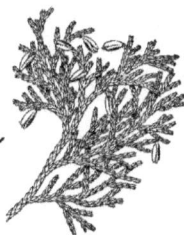

The First of February.

The birthday of St. Ignatius, bishop and martyr, who governed the church of Antioch, the third after the Apostle St. Peter. Being condemned to the beasts in the persecution of Trajan, he was by that emperor sent to Rome in chains, where in the presence of the Senate he was subjected to the most frightful torments, and delivered to the lions, which lacerated him with their teeth, and made of him a sacrifice to Christ.

The Second of February.

The Purification of the Blessed Virgin Mary or the Presentation of Jesus in the Temple, called by the Greeks Hypapante (meeting) of the Lord and by the people Candlemas. ✠ *Among those with the reputation of martyrdom, near Donaldsonville, Louisiana, Father Jean François Buisson de Saint-Come, of the Seminary of Quebec. After serving for a time at Mines, Nova Scotia, he was assigned to the western mission. He labored for a time at the Cahokia mission in Illinois, then he followed Fathers Montigny and Davion to the lower Mississippi and took up his residence amongst the Natchez. Shortly after he returned to the Tamaroa (opposite the present city of St. Louis) and preached to them, until he was relieved and again descended to the Natchez. To seek relief from a cruel illness, he started from his mission for Mobile, accompanied by three Frenchmen and a slave. While asleep at night on the bank of the river, the party was attacked and murdered by the Chitimacha about fifty miles from the mouth of the Mississippi. — At Rochester, Minnesota the birthday of the Servant of God Giancarlo Rastelli, cardiac surgeon and researcher at the Mayo Clinic in Rochester.*

The Third of February.

At Sebaste, in Armenia, in the time of the governor Agricolaus, the passion of St. Blaise, bishop and martyr, who after working many miracles, was scourged a long time, and suspended on a tree where he was lacerated with iron combs. He was then imprisoned in a dark dungeon, thrown into a lake from which he came out safe, and finally, by order of the same judge, he and two boys were beheaded. — The same day St. Ansgar, bishop of Bremen, who converted the Swedes and the Danes to the faith of Christ. ✝ *Among those with the reputation of sanctity, at Baltimore, Maryland the Servant of God Mother Mary Elizabeth Lange O.S.P., religious, foundress of the Oblate Sisters of Providence for the education and care of African Americans. Her cause was opened by William Cardinal Keeler.*

The Fourth of February.

At Sempringham, England, St. Gilbert, confessor and founder of the Gilbertine order. — At Florence, St. Andrew Corsini, bishop of Fiesole, whose birthday is the 6th of January. ✝ *Among those with the reputation of martyrdom, at Axacan (Occoquan) on the Rappahannock River, Virginia, the Jesuits Father Luis de Quiros and the lay brothers Gabriel de Solis and Juan Mendez. They had come to Virginia with the Vice Provincial P. Segura. When the missionaries found that their treacherous guide, Luis de Velasco, did not return to them, P. Quiros with his companions set out to effect a return of the misguided man by a personal conference. But Luis met them with hypocritical excuses. When the disconsolate missionaries turned to leave the village, the Indians rushed on them and killed them with a shower of arrows.*

The Fifth of February.

At Catania, in Sicily, in the time of the emperor Decius and the judge Quinctian, the birthday of St. Agatha, virgin and martyr. After being buffeted, imprisoned, tortured, racked, dragged over pieces of earthenware and burning coals, and having her breasts cut off, she consummated her sacrifice in prison while engaged in prayer. ✝ *Among those with the reputation of sanctity, at Reserve, Louisiana, the Servant of God Monsignor Jean Martin Eyraud, priest, beloved pastor of St. Peter Parish and mentor to young priests in the Archdiocese of New Orleans. His cause was approved by Pope John Paul II.*

The Sixth of February.

The Festival of St. Titus, bishop and confessor. — At Cæsarea, in Cappadocia, the birthday of St. Dorothy, virgin and martyr, who was stretched on the rack, then a long time scourged with boughs of the palm-tree, and finally condemned to capital punishment, under Sapricius, governor of that province. Her noble confession of Christ converted a lawyer named Theophilus, who was also tortured in a barbarous manner, and finally put to death by the sword. — At Nagasaki, Japan, Saints Paul Miki and companions, known as the Twenty-six Martyrs of Japan. They suffered under the daimyo Toyotomi Hideyoshi, who crucified them and pierced them with spears on the 5th of this month.

The Seventh of February.

The holy abbot St. Romuald, founder of the monks of Camaldoli, whose birthday is the 19th of June.

+ *Among those with the reputation of sanctity, at Rome, Italy the Servant of God Francis J. Parater, seminarian of the Diocese of Richmond, Virginia. His cause was deemed valid by Pope Benedict XVI.*

The Eighth of February.

At Rome, St. John de Matha, confessor, founder of the Order of the Most Holy Trinity for the redemption of captives, who reposed in the Lord on the 17th of December. — At Somasca, Italy, the birthday of St. Jerome Emiliani, confessor, founder of the Congregation of Somascha. Gaining renown for many miracles during his life and after his death, he was inscribed among the beatified by Benedict XIV and canonized by Clement XIII. — At Schio, Italy, the birthday of St. Josephine Bakhita, F.D.C.C., religious, a former slave known for her holiness of life. She was enrolled in the catalog of the saints by Pope John Paul II.

The Ninth of February.

At Alexandria in Egypt, St. Cyril, bishop and doctor of the church, a most celebrated defender of the Catholic faith, who rested in peace with a great reputation of learning and sanctity. In some places he is commemorated on this day, in many others on the 27th of June. —In the same city, in the reign of Decius, the birthday of St. Apollonia, virgin, who had all her teeth plucked out by the persecutors; then having constructed and lighted a pyre, they threatened to burn her alive, unless she repeated certain impious words after them. Deliberating awhile with herself, she suddenly slipped from their grasp, and feeling an inspiration of the Holy Ghost, rushed voluntarily into the fire that they had prepared. The very authors of her death were struck with terror at the sight of a woman who was more willing to die than they to condemn her.

✝ *Among those with the reputation of martyrdom, at Occoquan, on the Rappahannock River in Virginia, Father Juan Bautista de Segura, the novices Gabriel de Granada and Sancho de Zevellos and the lay brothers Cristóval Redondo and Pedro Linares. Father Segura had worked at various points along the coast of Florida, Georgia and the Carolinas, with little success. About to give up the impracticable field, he received orders from S. Pius V and S. Francis Borgia to persevere. Accompanied by a converted Indian chief, Luis de Velasco, Father Segura, Vice Provincial of Florida, with his companions (the reputed martyrs of February 4) and four Indian boys, sailed from S. Helena (St. Augustine), and landed near the present St. Mary's on the Chesapeake Bay. But their guide, a brother of the chief, apostatized, and the Indians, after having slain Father Quiros on the 4th of February, killed Father Segura and his companions, with the hatchets they had taken from them, on the ninth.*

The Tenth of February.

O n Monte Cassino, St. Scholastica, a virgin, whose soul her brother, St. Benedict, the abbot, saw leaving her body in the form of a dove, and ascending to heaven. ✝ *Among those with the reputation of sanctity, at Mesa, Arizona, the Servant of God Paul Michael Murphy, M.J., consecrated member of Miles Jesu.*

The death of Father Segura and companions

The Eleventh of February.

At Lourdes, in France, the apparition of the Blessed Virgin Immaculate.

The Twelfth of February.

In some places, the seven Holy Founders of the Order of Servites of the Blessed Virgin Mary, who are mentioned on the 17th of February.

The Thirteenth of February.

Among those with the reputation of martyrdom, at Huehuetenango, Guatemala, Brother James Alfred Miller F.S.C., religious, a missionary and educator who was shot by masked gunmen at the De La Salle Indian School.

The Fourteenth of February.

At Rome, on the Flaminian road, in the time of the emperor Claudius, the birthday of St. Valentine, priest and martyr, who after having cured and instructed many persons, was beaten with clubs and beheaded. — The birthday of St. Cyril, bishop, who with his brother St. Methodius, bishop, is in many places remembered this day, and in other places on the 7th of July.

The Fifteenth of February.

At Brescia, in the time of the emperor Hadrian, the birthday of the holy martyrs Sts. Faustinus and Jovita, who received the triumphant crown of martyrdom after many glorious combats for the faith of Christ.

The Sixteenth of February.

Among those with the reputation of sanctity, at Milwaukee, Wisconsin the Servant of God, Father Stephen Eckert, O.F.M. Cap., parish priest in New York and mission priest for African Americans at St. Benedict the Moor in Milwaukee. His cause was approved by Pope John Paul II.

The Seventeenth of February.

In Tuscany, on Mount Senario, the seven Holy Founders of the Order of Servites of the Blessed Virgin Mary. After a most austere kind of life, they died a death precious in the Lord, with a reputation for merits and prodigies. As one spirit of fraternal love united them in life, and as the people joined them together in the same veneration after death, Leo XIII placed them together in the catalogue of the Saints.

In many places they are venerated on this day, in others on the 12th of February. ✚ *Among those with the reputation of sanctity, at Passaic, New Jersey, the Servant of God, Archbishop Jan Cieplak, persecuted and imprisoned by the Bolshevik revolutionaries in Russia. His cause was opened on June 23, 1952.*

The Eighteenth of February.

At Jerusalem, the birthday of St. Simeon, bishop and martyr, who is said to have been the son of Cleophas, and a relative of the Saviour according to the flesh. He was consecrated bishop of Jerusalem after St. James, the brother of our Lord, and in the persecution of Trajan, after having endured many torments, he consummated his martyrdom. All who were present, even the judge himself, were astonished that a man one hundred and twenty years of age could bear the torment of crucifixion with such fortitude and constancy.

The Nineteenth of February.

Among those with the reputation of sanctity, at Dubuque, Iowa, the Servant of God Bishop Mathias Loras, the first bishop of the diocese of Dubuque and founder of missions and parishes.

The Twentieth of February.

Among those with the reputation of martyrdom, amongst the Fox tribe, in Wisconsin, the memory of Father Leonard Vatier, O.F.M.

The Twenty-first of February.

At Faenza, St. Peter Damian, Cardinal bishop of Ostia, and Doctor of the Church, celebrated for learning and sanctity. ✝ *Among those with the reputation of martyrdom, at Guangzhou, China the Servant of God Francis Xavier Ford, M.M., bishop of Meixian, beaten and died in prison at the hands of the Chinese Communists.*

The Twenty-second of February.

The Chair of the Apostle St. Peter. This festival was instituted to commemorate the establishment of the Holy See at Rome. ✝ *Among those with the reputation of martyrdom, at Hawikuh (Aguico), amongst the Zuñi Indians of New Mexico, Father Francisco Letrado, O.F.M. He asked his superiors at Mexico City to send him to the Zuñi mission because it was the most discouraging of all the missions in New Mexico. When, on Sunday, he urged his people to come and hear Mass, he was pierced by a shower of arrows.*

The Twenty-third of February.

In some churches, St. Peter Damian, bishop and doctor of the Church, whose birthday is on the 21st of February. — Also St. Polycarp, bishop and martyr, whose birthday is on the 26th of January. ✝ *Among those with the reputation of martyrdom, at Denver, Colorado, Father Leo Heinrichs, O.F.M. He was born at Oestrich, Germany, emigrated to New York, and entered the Order of St. Francis, in the province of the Holy Name at Paterson, N. J. Whilst distributing Holy Communion, he was shot by an Italian, in St. Elizabeth's Church, Denver, Colorado. —Among those with the reputation of sanctity, at Benton, Wisconsin, Venerable Father Samuel Charles Mazzuchelli, O.P. He was born in Milan, Italy and emigrated to Cincinnati, Ohio, where he was ordained. He served and founded numerous parishes and schools in Michigan, Wisconsin, and Iowa, served as a missionary to the Indians, and designed and built churches, most notably the Cathedral Church of the diocese of Dubuque. He also assisted in the founding of the Sisinisawa Dominican Sisters. Pope John Paul II declared his virtues heroic.*

The Twenty-fourth of February.

In Judea, the birthday of the Apostle St. Matthias, who was chosen by lot by the apostles after the Ascension of our Lord in the place of the traitor Judas, and suffered martyrdom for preaching the Gospel.

The Twenty-seventh of February.

At Isola, in the province of Abruzzi, St. Gabriel of the Sorrowful Virgin, confessor, and cleric of the Passionist congregation. Known for his merits during his short life and for miracles after death, Pope Benedict XV enrolled him in the catalogue of the saints. ✝ *Among those with the reputation of martyrdom, at Hawikuh in New Mexico, Father Martin de Arvide, O.F.M. He was killed by the Zipias Indians shortly after Father Francisco Letrado. — At St. Augustine, Florida, Venerable Father Felix Varela y Morales. He was born in Cuba and ordained a priest there. A noted professor and elected representative, he was sentenced to death by the Spanish crown. Emigrating to the United States in December 1823, he served in the Diocese of New York and became Vicar General. He was known for defending the rights of Irish immigrants and publishing Spanish-language periodicals and books. He retired to Florida where he died. Pope Benedict XVI declared his virtues heroic.*

Annunciation

St. Joseph

Crucifixion

St. Frances of Rome

St. Patrick

March

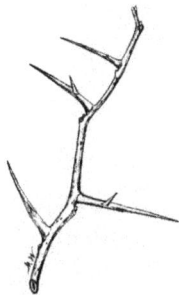

The First of March.

In Pembrokeshire in Wales, the birthday of St. David, confessor and bishop of Menevia, who was known for miracles and who was entered in the catalog of saints by Pope Callistus II.

The Second of March.

Among those with the reputation of martyrdom, in Florida, south of St. Augustine, a Franciscan Father and an Indian Chief. A chief had been converted by the Franciscans, on the eastern coast of Florida, but his tribe demanded that the chief should renounce his faith and put the friars to death. On his refusal they killed him and one of the Franciscans; two others escaped.

The Third of March.

At Bensalem, Pennsylvania, the birthday of Saint Katherine Drexel, S.B.S. Born to a wealthy Philadelphia family but moved by the plight of the American Indians, she contributed her money to the missions and saw the need for more missionaries to shoulder the work. She forsook society and entered the convent, founding the congregation of the

Sisters of the Blessed Sacrament, with its mission to the American Indians and to African Americans. The order's motherhouse was built in Bensalem, Pennsylvania. For the remainder of her life she spent her inheritance on the support of her work, founding dozens of schools and mission centers, often in the face of great racial hostility. She was raised to the altars by Pope John Paul II. ✝ *Among those with the reputation of martyrdom, in Upper Louisiana, Father Juan Mingues, O.F.M. He was killed in a massacre by Missouri Indians.*

The Fourth of March.

At Wilna, in Lithuania, St. Casimir, son of king Casimir, whom the Roman Pontiff, Leo X, placed in the number of the Saints. — At Rome, on the Appian way, during the persecution of Valerian, the birthday of St. Lucius, pope and martyr, who was first exiled for the faith of Christ; but being permitted by divine Providence to return to his church, he suffered martyrdom by decapitation, after having combated the Novatians. His praises have been published by St. Cyprian.

The Sixth of March.

The feast of the holy martyrs Perpetua and Felicity, who received the glorious crown of martyrdom on the 7th of this month.

St. Katherine Drexel
An original drawing by Lori Kauffmann

The Seventh of March.

In the monastery of Fossanova, near Terracina, St. Thomas Aquinas, confessor and doctor, of the Order of Preachers, illustrious by the nobility of his birth, the sanctity of his life, and his knowledge of theology. Leo XIII declared him heavenly patron of all Catholic schools.—In Carthage, Tunisia, in the reign of the emperor Severus, the birthday of the Saints Perpetua and Felicity, whose festival is kept by many on this day and by some on the 6th of this month. St. Augustine relates that Felicity, being with child, her execution was deferred according to law until after her delivery, and while she was in labor she mourned, and when exposed to the beasts she rejoiced.

✝ *Among those with the reputation of sanctity, at Saint Louis, Missouri, the Servant of God, Sister Theresia of the Holy Trinity, Carmel, D.C.J., religious.*

The Eighth of March.

At Granada, in Spain, St. John of God, founder of the Order of the Brothers Hospitallers, celebrated for his mercy to the poor, and his contempt of self. Pope Leo XIII declared him heavenly patron of hospitals and the infirm.

The Ninth of March.

At Rome, St. Frances, a widow, renowned for her noble extraction, holiness of life, and the gift of miracles.

The Tenth of March.

At Sebaste, in Armenia, forty holy martyrs. ✝ *Among those with the reputation of martyrdom, at Onondaga, in the present State of New York, Frances Gonanhatenha. Born at Onondaga, and converted by Father Fremin, with other Christians she had retired to Caughnawaga on the Canadian side of the St. Lawrence. She was a model of piety, modesty and charity. With her companions she was surprised by the Mohawks and English and tortured. Then she was brought to Onondaga, and, because she remained true to the faith, she was tortured again for three successive nights, then tied to the stake and, after being burned for a considerable time, scalped and forced to run till she fell beneath a shower of stones.*

The Twelfth of March.

At Rome, St. Gregory, pope and eminent doctor of the Church, who on account of his illustrious deeds, and the conversion of the English to the faith of Christ, was surnamed the Great, and called the Apostle of England.

St. Jean de Brébeuf

The Sixteenth of March.

At St. Ignace, in Ontario, the birthday of St. Jean de Brébeuf, missionary and martyr. He was captured with St. Gabriel Lalement during the Iroquois invasion of Huronia, tied to a stake, and beaten with clubs throughout his body. Among other torments, his captors poured boiling water on him, placed a collar of red-hot tomahawks around his neck, roasted him within a belt of pitch and bark, cut off his lips and tongue, and scalped him. Finally, his chest was cut open and his heart eaten, whence he went to his holy reward. His feast was established on the 26th of September by Pope Pius XI and moved to the 19th of October by Pope Paul VI. ✝ *Among those with the reputation of martyrdom, at the Mission of Santa Cruz, on the San Saba River, Texas, the Franciscan Fathers Alonzo Giraldo Terreros and José Santiestevan. Father Terreros was superior of the mission of San Saba. Some two thousand Comanche Indians, shouting and firing, surrounded the mission, demanding that the priest accompany them to the fort, a few miles off. He mounted a horse, but had ridden only a few feet, when he was shot; with a groan he fell dead from his horse. Then the Indians made a general attack, killing some of the soldiers stationed at the mission. Father Santiestevan fled to the storeroom, but that was the first place the assailants visited. He perished under the blows of their weapons. Father Miguel Molina was wounded, but escaped during the night. — Among those with the reputation of sanctity, at Manila, Philippines, Venerable Father Aloysius Schwartz, priest, missionary and founder of the Sisters of Mary of Banneux and Brothers of Christ.*

The Seventeenth of March.

In Ireland, the birthday of St. Patrick, bishop and confessor, who was the first to preach Christ in that country, and became illustrious by great miracles and virtues. — At St. Ignace in Ontario, the birthday of St. Gabriel Lalement, priest and martyr. Captured by the Iroquois with St. Jean de Brebeuf, he was bound to a post and burned all over his body, before his eyes were put out and hot coals placed in the sockets, among other torments. He was tomahawked and his heart cut from his chest, thus completing his martyrdom. He is honored with the other North American martyrs on the 26th of September or the 19th of October.

The Eighteenth of March.

At Jerusalem, St. Cyril, bishop and doctor, who suffered many injuries from the Arians for the faith. Often exiled from his church, he at length rested in peace with a great reputation for sanctity. A magnificent testimony of the purity of his faith is given by a general Council, in a letter to pope Damasus.

The Nineteenth of March.

In Judea, the birthday of St. Joseph, spouse of the Most Blessed Virgin Mary. Pius IX, yielding to the desires and prayers of the whole Catholic world, declared him Patron of the Universal Church.

The Twentieth of March.

Among those with the reputation of martydom, amongst the Tamarois Indians in Illinois, Father Gaston. He belonged to the Seminary of Quebec and had been ordained there. When Father Thaumur de la Source returned to Canada, Father Joseph Courrier and Father Gaston were sent to succeed him in 1730. The latter was killed by Indians soon after reaching Tamarois.

The Twenty-first of March.

On Monte Cassino, the birthday of the holy abbot St. Benedict, who restored and wonderfully extended in the West the monastic discipline, which was almost destroyed. His life, brilliant in virtues and miracles, was written by pope St. Gregory.

The Twenty-second of March.

At Madrid, St. Isidore, a laborer. He reposed in the Lord on the 15th of May.

The Twenty-third of March.

At Lima, in Peru, the archbishop St. Turibius of Mogrovejo, through whose labors faith and ecclesiastical discipline were diffused through America.

The Twenty-fourth of March.

The Feast of St. Gabriel the Archangel, who was sent by God to announce the Incarnation of the Divine Word. ✝ *Among those with the reputation of martyrdom, at Fort St. Louis, Texas, the Recollect Missionaries Zenobius Membré and Maxime LeClerq, and the Sulpician Chefdeville. Father Zenobius was born in France and was a member of the Franciscan province of St. Anthony. Membre with two Franciscans and three Sulpicians followed La Salle into Texas. The commander erected Fort St. Louis on Espiritu Santo Bay and left there Fathers Membre, LeClerq and Chefdeville with 20 persons. Having failed in establishing a mission amongst the Indians, the three priests with the garrison were killed and the fort burned by the Karankawas. — Among those with the reputation of sanctity, at Miami, Florida, the Servant of God Father John Joseph McKniff, O.S.A., missionary and pastor in Cuba and Peru.*

The Twenty-fifth of March.

The Annunciation of the most Blessed Virgin Mary, Mother of God. ✝ *Among those with the reputation of martyrdom, near Fulton, Hawamba Co., Mississippi, the Jesuit missionary P. Antonin Senat. When the massacre at Natchez involved the valley of the Mississippi in Indian wars, an expedition of French and Illinois was sent against the Chickasaws, and Father Senat accompanied the force as chaplain. After some success the French corps, which was to cooperate with another from the south, was attacked by the whole Chickasaw army. Vincennes, the commander, d'Artaguiette, Father Senat and others were taken.*

The missionary could readily have escaped. He would not, however, abandon those who needed his ministry. The prisoners were tied by fours to stakes and put to death with all the refinement of cruelty, on Palm Sunday. To the last the devoted Jesuit exhorted his companions to suffer with patience and courage, to honor their religion and country.

The Twenty-seventh of March.

In some churches, the festival of St. John Damascene, priest and Father of the Church, who defended sacred icons. His feast was moved by Pope Paul VI to his birthday on the 4th of December.

The Twenty-eighth of March.

Near Villack, in Hungary, St. John of Capistrano, confessor, of the order of Minorites, illustrious by the sanctity of his life, and his zeal for the propagation of the Catholic faith. By his prayers and miracles, he routed a most powerful army of Turks and forced them to raise the seige of Belgrade. His birthday is on the 23rd of October.

The Thirtieth of March.

Among those with a reputation of sanctity, at Boulder Creek, California, the Servant of God Cora Louise Evans, visionary and promoter of the mystical humanity of Christ. Her cause was approved by Pope Benedict XVI.

St. Isidore

St. Mark

Resurrection

St. Anselm

St. Catherine of Siena

April

The Second of April.

St. Francis of Paola, founder of the Order of Minims. As he was renowned for virtues and miracles, he was inscribed among the saints by Leo X. — At Tumon, Guam, St. Pedro Calungsod, martyr. Born on a Philippine island (likely Cebu, Bohol, or Leyte) he served at the altar as a young man and accompanied the Jesuits to the Mariana Islands. Together with Blessed Father Diego Luis de San Vitores, he arrived at Tumon, Guam on April 2, 1672. The village chief there, Matapang, had been baptized but became hostile to the faith. When his Christian wife allowed the missionaries to baptize his daughter, Matapang became enraged. He speared the youth and finished him with a machete blow to the head, after which he killed the priest and then sank their bodies in the ocean. Calungsod was canonized by Pope Benedict XVI. — At Tumon, Guam, the birthday of Blessed Father Diego Luis de San Vitores, S.J., martyr. His memory is kept on October 6.

The Fourth of April.

At Seville, in Spain, St. Isidore, a bishop eminent for sanctity and learning, who shed lustre on his country by his zeal for the Catholic faith, and the observance of ecclesiastical discipline.

The Fifth of April.

At Vannes, in Brittany, St. Vincent Ferrer, confessor, of the Order of Preachers, who was mighty in word and deed, and converted many thousands of infidels to Christ.

The Seventh of April.

The birthday of St. John Baptist de la Salle, priest and confessor. In many places he is honored on this day, and in others on the 15th of May. ✝ *Among those reputed for their sanctity, at Brooklyn, New York the Servant of God Monsignor Bernard J. Quinn, priest and founder of St. Peter Claver parish and the Little Flower Orphanage.*

The Eleventh of April.

At Rome, St. Leo, pope and confessor, who was surnamed the Great on account of his extra-ordinary merits. He gave the seal of his authority to the holy council of Chalcedon, which was held in his time and which condemned Eutyches through his legates. After having merited the gratitude of the Church of God and the whole flock of Christ by the many decrees which he issued and the many excellent treatises which he wrote, this good and zealous shepherd rested in peace. His birthday is on the 10th of November. —The birthday of St. Stanislaus, bishop and martyr. In many places he is honored on this day, in others on the 7th of May. ✝ *Among those reputed for their sanctity, at Allentown, Pennsylvania, the birthday of the Servant of God Mother Therese of Jesus, foundress of the Carmelite Nuns of the Ancient Observance of Allentown.*

The Thirteenth of April.

At Seville, in Spain, St. Hermenegild, son of Leovigild, Arian king of the Visigoths, who was incarcerated for the confession of the Catholic faith. By order of his wicked father he was beheaded because he had refused to receive Communion from an Arian bishop, on the Paschal solemnity, and thus exchanging an earthly for a heavenly kingdom, he entered the abode of the blessed, both as a king and a martyr. — In many places, the feast of St. Martin, pope and martyr, who is in others honored on the 12th of November.

The Fourteenth of April.

At Rome, St. Justin, martyr, the Philosopher, who had addressed to the emperors his second Apology in defense of our religion, and upheld it by strong arguments. Being accused of professing Christianity by the intrigues of the Cynic Crescens, whose conduct and immorality he had reproved, he obtained the reward of a martyr, as a remuneration for his faithful confession. — At Rome, on the Appian way, the birthday of the holy martyrs Tiburtius, Valerian, and Maximus, who suffered in the time of the emperor Alexander and the prefect Almachius. The first two being converted to Christ by the exhortations of blessed Cecilia, and baptized by pope St. Urban, were beaten with rods, and decapitated for the true faith. But Maximus, chamberlain of the prefect, moved by their constancy, and encouraged by the vision of an angel, believed in Christ, and was scourged with leaded whips until he expired. ✝ *Among those with the reputation of sanctity, the Servant of God, Bishop James Anthony Walsh, titular bishop of Seine-Assuan and co-founder of the Catholic Foreign Mission Society of America, also known as the Maryknoll Fathers and Brothers.*

The Fifteenth of April.

The birthday of St. Damien de Veuster of Molokai, SS.CC. His memory is kept on this day in the Diocese of Honolulu and on May 10 elsewhere. + *Among those with the reputation of sanctity, at Grajal de Campos, Spain, the Servant of God, Maria Adelaida of Saint Teresa O.C.D., religious of the Discalced Carmelite Nuns.*

The Sixteenth of April.

Among those with the reputation of sanctity, at San Juan, Puerto Rico, the Servant of God Brother Ninfas Victorino F.S.C., religious, educator and founder of the Young Cuban Catholics Federation. His cause was opened on September 8, 2000.

The Seventeenth of April.

At Caughnawaga, Canada, the birthday of Saint Kateri Tekakwitha, Virgin, the "Lily of the Mohawks." Her memory is kept on the 14th of July. —At Rome, St. Anicetus, pope and martyr, who obtained the palm of martyrdom in the persecution of Marcus Aurelius Antoninus. + *Among those with the reputation of sanctity, at Chicago, Illinois, the memory of Venerable Mother Maria Kaupas, S.S.C., foundress. She emigrated from Lithuania to Scranton, Pennsylvania. She took religious vows and founded the Sisters of St. Casimir there to educate Lithuanian immigrants, and she also established the order's motherhouse in Chicago. Pope Benedict XVI declared her virtues heroic.*

The Eighteenth of April.

Among those with the reputation of martyrdom, at Carniceria, Texas, Brother José Pita O.F.M. When Father Antonio Margil restored the missions in Texas, Brother Pita, thinking that the presence of troops had made travel safe, undertook to reach the mission for which he had volunteered, without the proper escort. At a place which has since borne the name of Carniceria, about 60 miles from San Xavier River, and on a site on which subsequently a mission was erected, he fell into an ambuscade of Lipan Apaches. He might have escaped, but to deliver a soldier, he begged the Indians to turn on him; but they killed him and his companion. He was the first Spanish Religious who died by the hands of Indians in that province. — Among those with the reputation of sanctity, at St. Leonards-on-Sea, Sussex, England, Venerable Mother Cornelia Connelly S.H.C.J., Foundress. She was born Cornelia Peacock to a Protestant family in Philadelphia. She married the Episcopal minister Pierce Connelly, and both were received into the Catholic Church soon after. When he decided to seek the priesthood, he requested Cornelia to enter the convent. She did so, and the next year she founded the Society of the Holy Child Jesus in England. Her husband, however, soon repudiated his priesthood and the faith and tried to wrest control of her order from her, but she remained steadfast and continued in her mission to educate the poor. Her virtues were proclaimed heroic by Pope John Paul II.

The Nineteenth of April.

Among those with the reputation of martyrdom, at Cicuye (Pecos), New Mexico, Brother Luis de Ubeda (or Escalona), O.F.M. He was a member of the Mexican province of the Holy Gospel and accompanied Coronado on his march to the Northwest, together with Father Juan de Padilla and Father Juan de la Cruz. He was appointed to instruct the Indians at Cicuye. When Coronado gave up New Mexico in disgust, Brother Luis remained at his pueblo, where the Indians had assigned him a little hut outside the village. From there he visited the neighboring pueblos. His exact fate is not known, but after the soldiers of Coronado had left, it is regarded as certain that he became a martyr.

The Twentieth of April.

Among those with the reputation of martyrdom, near De Pere, Wisconsin, Brother Louis Le Boesme, S.J. Born at Saintes, France, he entered the Society of Jesus in the province of Toulouse, whence he came to Canada. He was given as a companion to the Indian missionary, Father Jean Injalran, S.J. and was martyred by the Winnebagos.

The Twenty-first of April.

At Canterbury, in England, St. Anselm, bishop and Doctor of the Church, who was renowned for sanctity and learning.

The Twenty-second of April.

At Rome, on the Appian way, the birthday of St. Soter, pope and martyr. — In the same city, pope St. Caius, who was crowned with martyrdom, under the emperor Diocletian.

The Twenty-third of April.

The birthday of St. George, whose illustrious martyrdom is honored by the Church of God among the combats of other crowned martyrs. — In Prussia, the birthday of St. Adalbert, bishop of Prague, and martyr, who preached the Gospel to the Poles and Hungarians. ✚ *Among those with the reputation of sanctity, at San Juan, Puerto Rico, the Servant of God Mother Soledad Sanjurjo, religious of the servants of Mary of the Ministers of the Sick.*

The Twenty-fourth of April.

At Sevis, in Switzerland, St. Fidelis of Sigmaringen, of the Order of Capuchin Minorites, who was sent thither to preach the Catholic faith. He was put to death by the heretics, and was placed among the holy martyrs by the Sovereign Pontiff, Benedict XIV. — At Angers in France, St. Mary Euphrasia Pelletier, virgin and foundress of the Institute of the Good Shepherd Sisters, whom Pius XII, Sovereign Pontiff, enrolled among the number of the saints.

The Twenty-fifth of April.

At Alexandria, the birthday of blessed Mark, evangelist, disciple and interpreter of the apostle St. Peter. He wrote his gospel at the request of the faithful of Rome, and taking it with him, proceeded to Egypt and founded a church at Alexandria, where he was the first to announce Christ. Afterwards, being arrested for the faith, he was bound, dragged over stones and endured great afflications. Finally he was confined to prison, where, being comforted by the visit of an angel, and even by an apparition of our Lord himself, he was called to the heavenly kingdom in the eighth year of the reign of Nero.

The Twenty-sixth of April.

At Rome, the birthday of blessed Cletus, pope who governed the Church the second after the apostle St. Peter, and was crowned with martyrdom in the persecution of Domitian. — In the same city, in the time of Maximiam, St. Marcellinus, pope and martyr, who was beheaded for the faith of Christ, with Claudius, Cyrinus, and Antoninus. So great was the persecution at this time that within a month seventeen thousand Christians were crowned with martyrdom. +

Among those with the reputation of martyrdom, at Massacre Island, Louisiana, Father Jacques Gravier S.J. He was born at Moulins, France, joined the Jesuits at Paris, and came to Quebec, whence he went to Michilimackinac. He succeeded Allouez in the Illinois mission begun by Marquette and is the true founder of that mission, where he spent ten years of incredible hardship and suffering. He first reduced the Illinois language to grammatical rules. Kaskaskia and Peoria Indians he grouped near Fort St. Louis on the Illinois River and despite the machinations of the medicine men moulded his flock into a model Christian church. Returning to the Peorias after other travels, he was attacked by them by a shower of arrows. One flint-headed weapon pierced his ear, but another struck him at the elbow and could not be extracted. He sought relief at Mobile, and even at Paris, but eventually died of his wounds.

The Twenty-seventh of April.

At Fribourg, Switzerland, St. Peter Canisius, priest of the Society of Jesus, confessor and doctor of the Church, who departed to the Lord on the 21st of December.

The Twenty-eighth of April.

At Rome, St. Paul of the Cross, a man remarkable for innocence of life and for the spirit of penance, and Founder of the Congregation of the Cross and Passion of our Lord Jesus Christ. Consumed with a burning love for Christ crucified, illustrious by his heavenly gifts and the working of miracles, and blessed with a perfect and finished virtue, he went to his repose in the Lord on the 18th of October. — On Futuna

Island, in Polynesia, the birthday of St. Peter Chanel, Marist priest, missionary and martyr who, by order of king Niuliki of Futuna, was killed with an axe. — At Saint-Laurent-sur-Sèvre, France, the birthday of St. Louis de Montfort, priest and confessor, renowned for his preaching and his devotion to the Blessed Virgin Mary.

The Twenty-ninth of April.

At Milan, St. Peter, martyr, of the order of Preachers, slain by the heretics for the Catholic faith. — The birthday of St. Catherine of Siena. In many places she is honored on this day, in others on the following day.

The Thirtieth of April.

At Rome, St. Catherine of Siena, virgin, of the Order of St. Dominic, renowned for her life and miracles. She was inscribed among the canonized virgins by Pius II. — In many places, the feast of St. Pius V, pope, who entered heaven on the following day, May 1st. He is honored in some places on the 5th of May.

Ascension

Sts. Philip and James

Pentecost

St. Athanasius

St. Philip Neri

May

The First of May.

The feast of St. Joseph the Worker, Spouse of the Blessed Virgin Mary, instituted by Pius XII. ✠ *Among those with the reputation of martyrdom, at Quivira, in Nebraska or Kansas, the memory of Father Juan de Padilla, O.F. M., the Protomartyr of the United States of America. He was born in Andalusia, Spain. After a short military career he took the habit of St. Francis, came to Mexico and joined the province of the Holy Gospel at Mexico City, serving as military chaplain and missionary. With Coronado, he penetrated as far north as Quivira, to the lower Loup River in Nebraska. Father Padilla evangelized the Indians about the present town of St. Paul, Howard County, with good success. When, however, he attempted the conversion of the Kaws, or Kansas, on his way south, he was attacked somewhere in Hall County, Nebraska and was slain. His companions escaped. Some believe that not St. Paul, Nebraska, but Junction City, Kansas, marks the site of Quivira and a monument has been erected there to Father Padilla.*

The Second of May.

At Alexandria, the birthday of St. Athanasius, bishop of that city and Doctor of the Church, most celebrated for sanctity and learning. Although almost all the world had formed a conspiracy to persecute him, he courageously defended the Catholic faith, from the reign of Constantine to that of Valens, against emperors, governors, and a multitude of Arian bishops, whose perfidious attacks forced him to wander as an exile over the whole earth without finding a place of security. At length, however, he was restored to his church, and after fighting many combats, and winning many crowns by his patience, he departed for heaven in the forty-sixth year of his priesthood, in the time of the emperors Valentinian and Valens.

The Third of May.

The blessed apostles Philip and James. Philip, after having converted nearly all Scythia to the faith of Christ, went to Hierapolis, in Asia, where he was fastened to a cross, overwhelmed with stones, and thus terminated his life gloriously. James, who is also called the brother of our Lord, was the first bishop of Jerusalem. Being hurled down from a pinnacle of the temple, he had his legs broken, and being then struck on the head with a dyer's staff, he expired, and was buried near the temple. — At Rome, on the Nomentan road, the holy martyrs Alexander, pope, Eventius and Theodulus, priests. Alexander was bound, imprisoned, racked, lacerated with hooks, burned, pierced in all his limbs with pointed instruments, and finally put to death, under the emperor Hadrian and the judge Aurelian. Eventius and Theodulus, after a long imprisonment, were exposed to the flames, and then beheaded.

The Fourth of May.

At Ostia, the birthday of St. Monica, mother of blessed Augustine, who has left us in the ninth book of his Confession a beautiful sketch of her life. — The memory of the Forty Martyrs of England and Wales, who won their crowns during the persecutions of the Reformation under the Tudor and Stuart kings. — In Puerto Rico, the memory of Blessed Carlos Manuel Rodríguez Santiago, elsewhere remembered on his birthday, July 13.

The Fifth of May.

At Rome, pope St. Pius V, of the Order of Preachers, who labored zealously and successfully for the reestablishment of ecclesiastical discipline, the extirpation of heresies, the destruction of the enemies of the Christian name, and governed the Catholic Church by holy laws and the example of a saintly life.

The Sixth of May.

Among those with the reputation of sanctity, at Loretto, Pennsylvania, the Servant of God Demetrius Augustine Gallitzin, priest, a Russian nobleman and missionary known as the "Apostle of the Alleghenies". His cause was opened in the diocese of Altoona-Johnstown by Bishop Joseph V. Adamec.

The Seventh of May.

At Cracow, in Poland, the birthday of St. Stanislaus, bishop and martyr, who was murdered by the wicked king Boleslaus.

The Eighth of May.

Among those with the reputation of sanctity, at Elizabeth, New Jersey, the memory of Venerable Sister Miriam Teresa Demjanovich, SC. She was born to Ruthenian immigrants in Bayonne, New Jersey. After a secular education, she became a Sister of Charity of Saint Elizabeth. Her spiritual director finding her of remarkable faith and intelligence, he bade her to write a series of conferences for her order, compiled under the title "Greater Perfection". She died only 2 years after her profession. Pope Benedict XVI declared her virtues heroic.

The Ninth of May.

At Nazianzus, the birthday of St. Gregory, bishop and doctor of the church, surnamed the Theologian, because of his remarkable knowledge of divinity. At Constantinople, he restored the Catholic faith, which was fast waning, and repressed the rising heresies.

The Tenth of May.

At Kalaupapa, Hawai'i, the memory of St. Damien de Veuster, SS.CC., priest, styled "the Apostle of Lepers". He was born January 3, 1840 in Tremelo, Belgium and joined the Congregation of the Sacred Hearts of Jesus and Mary in 1860. Desiring to be sent to a mission, he arrived on the island of Hawai'i in 1864, where he was stationed at the mission of North Kohala. An outbreak of leprosy caused the Hawaiian government to quarantine sufferers of the disease on the Kalaupapa peninsula of Molokai, but problems soon arose in the quarantine community. Father Damien and three other priests volunteered to minister to it notwithstanding the danger, and after his arrival in 1873 he built the Parish of St. Philomena and tended to the inhabitants' spiritual and physical needs. Eleven years later he himself contracted leprosy, but only accelerated his labors as a result. He finally died of the

St. Damien de Veuster of Molokai

disease on April 15, 1889, on which day his memory is
still kept in Hawai'i. He was beatified on June 4, 1995
by Pope John Paul II and canonized October 11, 2009
by Pope Benedict XVI. — At Florence, the bishop
St. Antoninus, of the Order of Preachers, renowned
for holiness and learning, whose birthday is on the 2nd
of May.

The Eleventh of May.

In some places, the feast of the blessed Apostles
Philip and James. ✝ *Among those with the reputation
of martyrdom, at Candelaria, Texas, the Franciscan missionary
José Francisco de Ganzabal. He had charge of the mission of San
Ildefonso in the time of Governor Pedro del Barrio Junco y Espriela.
On Ascension Day, Father Ganzabal went to pass the festival with
his fellow Religious at Candelaria. At nightfall three Fathers were
in the little room at the mission and a Spaniard was standing at the
door, when some Coco Indians fired and killed the Spaniard, who fell
at the feet of one of the Fathers. The missionary hastened to aid him,
but when Father de Ganzabal called out to learn who the assailants
were, he received an arrow through his heart.*

The Twelfth of May.

At Rome, on the Ardeatine road, the holy martyrs
Nereus and Achilleus, brothers, who first
underwent a long exile for Christ in the island of
Pontia with Flavia Domitilla, whose chamberlains

they were. Afterwards they endured a most severe scourging. Finally, as the ex-consul Minutius Rufus endeavored by using the rack and fire to force them to offer sacrifices, they said, that having been baptized by the blessed Apostle Peter, they could by no means sacrifice to idols. They were beheaded, and their sacred relics, with those of Flavia Domitilla, were, by order of pope Clement VIII, solemnly transferred the day before this, from the sacristty of St. Adrian to their ancient church now repaired, in which they were formerly preserved. — In the same place, on the Aurelian road, the holy martyr St. Pancras, who, at fourteen years of age, endured martyrdom by decapitation under Diocletian. ✝ *Among those with the reputation of martyrdom, at Puaray, New Mexico, Father Francisco Lopez, O.F.M. He was a native of Sevilla and, when 17 years old, took the habit of St. Francis at Xeres de la Frontera. As superior of the mission band of Brother Agustin Ruiz, he was sent to New Mexico where he set up his headquarters at Puaray, the principal town of the Tiguez Indians, opposite Bernalillo. The soldiers, under Chamuscado, having explored the neighborhood, returned to Mexico; the Friars, however, P. Lopez, P. Juan de S. Maria and Brother Ruiz remained at Puaray. In the spring following the departure of Father Juan, Father Lopez, while praying near the pueblo, was killed with two blows of a wooden warclub by a Tigua Indian. In February, his relics were found by P. Estevan de Perea, and transferred to the church of Sandia, where miracles are attributed to him.*

The Thirteenth of May.

At Fatima, Spain, the apparition of Our Lady to Lucia Santos and Jacinta and Francisco Marto. — In some places is kept the feast of St. Robert Bellarmine, of the Society of Jesus, cardinal and one time bishop of Capua, confessor and doctor of the Church. His birthday is on the 17th of September.

The Fourteenth of May.

The birthday of Saint Mother Théodore Guérin, S.P., foundress. Her memory is kept on October 3. — In many places, the feast of the Apostle St. Matthias, who is honored elsewhere on the 24th of February. — The birthday of the holy martyr Boniface, who suffered at Tarsus, in Cilicia, under Diocletian and Maximian. His body was subsequently carried to Rome, and buried on the Latin road.

The Fifteenth of May.

At Rouen, St. John Baptist de la Salle, confessor, who deserved well both of religion and society by his labors for the education of youth, especially of the poor, and by the founding of the Society of the Brothers of the Christian schools. — At Madrid, St. Isidore, a laborer. Being renowned for miracles, pope Gregory XV placed him in the number of the saints at the same time with St. Ignatius, St. Francis, St. Theresa, and St. Philip. He is honored in many places on this day, and in others on the 22nd of March.

✝ *Among those with the reputation of sanctity, at Berlin, Germany, the Servant of God Monsignor Edward Joseph Flanagan, priest and founder of the Boys' Town orphanage near Omaha Nebraska. — At Santa Maria Magdalena, Mexico, the Servant of God Father Eusebio Kino, S.J., scholar and founder of missions in Arizona, most notably San Xavier del Bac near Tucson.*

The Sixteenth of May.

At Gubbio, St. Ubald, a bishop renowned for his miracles.

The Seventeenth of May.

At Villareal, in the kingdom of Valencia, St. Pascal of the Order of Minorites, a man remarkable for innocence of life and the spirit of penance. Pope Leo XIII declared him heavenly patron of Eucharistic Congresses and Societies formed in honor of the Most Blessed Sacrament.

The Eighteenth of May.

At Camerino, the holy martyr Venantius, who at fifteen years of age, with ten others, ended a glorious combat by being beheaded under the emperor Decius and the governor Antiochus. — The birthday of St. John, pope and martyr, who was called to Ravenna by the Arian king of Italy, Theodoric, and after languishing a long time in prison for the orthodox faith, departed his life. He is honored on this day in many places, in others on the 27th of May.

The Nineteenth of May.

The birthday of St. Peter of Morrone, who, while leading the life of an anchoret, was created Sovereign Pontiff and called Celestine V. Having abdicated the pontificate, he led a religious life in solitude, where, renowned for virtues and miracles, he went to God. — The holy bishops of England, St. Dunstan of Canterbury, whose birthday is this day; St. Ethelwold of Winchester who went to the Lord on the 1st of August; and St. Oswald of Worcester who passed into heaven on the 29th of February.

The Twentieth of May.

At Aquila, in Abruzzo, St. Bernardine of Siena, of the Order of Minorites, who ennobled Italy by his preaching and example. + *Among those with the reputation of martyrdom, at the pueblo of Santiago, amongst the Tigua Indians, New Mexico, Brother Augustin Rodriguez (Ruiz), O.F.M. He was a native of Spain had taken the habit in the province of the Holy Gospel at Mexico City, but asked to be transferred to the custody of San Francisco de Zacatecas to teach catechism to the Indians and gain the crown of martyrdom. He was sent to the exposed mission of the valley of San Bartolo, in the vicinity of Allende (Chihuahua), where he led a life of austere asceticism. After having visited the Indians, north of the Rio Grande near El Paso, he organized a missionary band, consisting of Father Francisco Lopez, Father Juan de S. Maria and himself. After Fathers Juan and Francisco had lost their lives, he also was killed by a Tehua Indian at Santiago near Puaray. The Indian threw his body into the river.*

The Twenty-first of May.

At Totatiche, Mexico, the memory of St. Christopher Magellanes, priest and martyr. Under the persecution of president Plutarco Calles, he was put to death by firing squad without trial on the 25th of this month.

The Twenty-second of May.

At Cascia, in Italy, St. Rita, a widow, and nun of the Order of Augustinians, who after being disengaged from the earthly marriage, loved only Christ, her eternal spouse.

The Twenty-third of May.

Among those with the reputation of sanctity, at Pyoktong, North Korea, the Servant of God Father Emil Kapaun, priest, decorated military chaplain and prisoner of war. His cause was opened in the Diocese of Wichita by Bishop Michael Jackels.

The Twenty-fourth of May.

Among those with the reputation of sanctity, at Gran Quivira, New Mexico, the Venerable servant of God, Maria Jesus de Agreda, Abbess of the Nuns of the Immaculate Conception at Agreda in Spain. Father Juan de Salas, O.F.M., went to the Xumana Indians, New Mexico, to bear the light of the gospel to them. To his surprise he found the Xumanas familiar with the Christian doctrines; they declared that they had been instructed in the faith of Christ by a woman. When Father Alonzo de Benavides returned to Spain, he learnt at the convent of the Ven. Maria de Agreda that she had in ecstasy visited New Mexico and instructed Indians there. The Franciscan writers from this time speak of this marvelous conversion of the Xumanas by the instrumentality of Maria de Agreda, as a settled fact. The Xumana nation, since, has been wasted away by wars and absorbed in some one of the New Mexican tribes.

The Twenty-fifth of May.

At Salerno, Italy, the demise of the blessed pope Gregory VII, a most zealous protector and champion of ecclesiastical liberty.— At Paris, St. Madeleine-Sophie Barat, foundress of the Congregation of the Sisters of the Sacred Heart, who was added to the list of holy virgins by Pope Pius XI. — At Florence, Italy, the birthday of

St. Mary Magdelen de Pazzi, virgin, of the Order of
the Carmelites, illustrious by the holiness of her life.
In many places she is honored on this day, in others
on the 29th of this month. — In many places, the
memory of the Venerable Bede, priest, whose birthday
is on the following day.

The Twenty-sixth of May.

At Rome, St. Philip Neri, founder of the
Congregation of the Oratory, celebrated for his
virginal purity, the gift of prophecy, and miracles. —
Also at Rome, St. Eleutherius, pope and martyr, who
converted many noble Romans to the Christian faith.
He sent the saints Damian and Fugatius to England,
who baptized king Lucius with his wife and almost all
his people.

The Twenty-seventh of May.

At Canterbury, in England, St. Augustine, bishop,
who was sent thither with others by the blessed
pope Gregory and preached the Gospel of Christ
to the English nation. Celebrated for virtues and
miracles, he went peacefully to his rest in the Lord. In
many places he is honored on this day, in others on the
following day. — At Jarrow, in England, the demise
of the Venerable Bede, priest, confessor and doctor,
renowned for sanctity and learning. In some places he

is remembered on this day, but in many others on the previous.— In some places, the feast of St. John, pope and martyr.

The Twenty-eighth of May.

St. Augustine, bishop of Canterbury and apostle to the English. He is honored by some on this day and by many others on the day previous.

The Twenty-ninth of May.

In some places, the memory of St. Mary Magdalen de Pazzi, virgin, whose birthday is on the 25th of this month.

The Thirtieth of May.

At Mexico City, Mexico, the birthday of St. Juan Diego to whom appeared Our Lady of Guadalupe. His feast is celebrated on December 9. — At Rome, on the Aurelian road, the birthday of St. Felix, pope and martyr, who was crowned with martyrdom under the emperor Aurelian.

The Thirty-first of May.

The feast of the Visitation of the Blessed Virgin Mary, or that of the Queenship of the Blessed Virgin Mary.

Corpus Christi

Nativity of St. John the Baptist

Trinity Sunday

St. Peter

St. Paul

June

The First of June.

At Brescia, Italy, St. Angela Merici, virgin, foundress of the Order of Nuns of St. Ursula, whose principal aim is to direct young girls in the ways of the Lord. Her birthday is on the 27th of January. — In many places, the feast of St. Justin Martyr, who is in others honored on the 14th of April.

The Second of June.

At Rome, the birthday of the holy martyr Marcellinus, priest, and Peter, exorcist, who instructed in the faith many persons detained in prison. Under Diocletian, they were loaded with chains, and, after enduring many torments, were beheaded by the judge Serenus, in a place which was then called the Black Forest, but which was in their honor afterwards known as the White Forest. Their bodies were buried in a crypt near St. Tiburtius, and pope St. Damasus composed for their tomb an epitaph in verse. — In Campania, during the reign of Decius, St. Erasmus, bishop and martyr, who was first scourged with leaded whips and then severely beaten with rods; he had also rosin, brimstone, lead, pitch, wax, and oil poured over him, without receiving any injury. Afterwards, under

Maximian, he was again subjected to most horrible tortures at Mola, but was still preserved from death by the power of God for the strengthening of others in the faith. Finally, celebrated for his sufferings, and called by God, he closed his life by a peaceful and holy end. His body was afterwards transferred to Gaeta. ✝ *Among those with the reputation of sanctity, at San Pedro, California, Father Patrick Peyton, C.S.C., known as the "Rosary priest" and founder of the Family Rosary Crusade.*

The Third of June.

At Namugongo in Uganda, Sts. Charles Lwanga and companions. Under the persecution of King Mwanga II, and after refusing to accede to his depravity, they were burned alive and thus entered their glory.

The Fourth of June.

At Agnone, Italy, St. Francis, of the noble Neapolitan family of the Caracciolos, confessor, and founder of the Congregation of the Minor Clerks Regular, who burned with an admirable love of God and his neighbor, and a most ardent desire to propagate devotion to the most holy Eucharist. His body is religiously honored at Naples. He was inscribed on the catalogue of the saints by Pius VII. ✝ *Among those with the reputation of martyrdom, at San Cristoval de Tanos, New*

Mexico, Fathers José de Arbizu and Antonio Carbonel, O.F.M. Don Diego de Vargas reasserted Spanish rule in New Mexico, where the churches had been destroyed and the missionaries martyred. But the Taos, Picuries, Tehuas, Tanos, Queres and Jemes Indians again rose in rebellion. Their first act was to profane the churches, the next to butcher the missionaries. At San Cristóval de Tanos they killed Father Joseph and Father Antony, missionaries of the Taos.

The Fifth of June.

St. Boniface, bishop of Mayence, who came from England to Rome, and was sent by Gregory II to Germany to preach the faith of Christ to the people of that country. Having converted large multitudes to the Christian religion, especially in Friesland, he merited the title of Apostle of the Germans. Being finally put to the sword by the furious Gentiles, he consummated his martyrdom with Eobanus and some other servants of God. ✝ *Among those with the reputation of martyrdom, amongst the Jemes Indians in New Mexico, Father Francis of Jesus Maria Casañas, O.F.M. He had worked amongst the Asinais Indians in Texas and had been sent by the other missionaries to Mexico to obtain a regular establishment of the Texas mission by royal order. At the reestablishment of the missions in New Mexico he accompanied the new custos, P. Salvador de San Antonio to Santa Fe and was sent to the pueblo of the Jemes. When a rebellion broke out, he was lured out of the village by some pagans, under the pretext that a dying man wished a priest to hear his confession. Then the war chief of the pueblo and the interpreter killed him with their clubs, the holy missionary repeating the names of Jesus and Mary till he expired.*

The Sixth of June.

St. Norbert, bishop of Magdeburg, founder of the Premonstratensian Order. ✝ *Among those with the reputation of martyrdom, at Fort St. Charles, Minnesota, Father Jean Pierre Aulneau, S.J. Born in France, at Moutiers-sur-Hay, he arrived at Quebec, and was sent to the West to study the languages of the Cree and Assiniboin nations and to push on farther to the Mandan Indians. He reached the Lake of the Woods and spent the winter in Fort Charles. Dispatched to Mackinac three canoes with a party of Frenchmen to secure provisions and ammunition, after one day's journey they were surprised by a party of Sioux Indians and murdered, on Massacre Island, in Canadian waters, to the southeast of Fort Charles. Their bodies were found September 17, 1736, and interred in the chapel of Fort Charles on September 18, of the same year. The remains of Father Aulneau and his companions were discovered in the summer.*

The Eighth of June.

Among those with the reputation of martyrdom, at San Ildefonso, New Mexico, Fathers Francisco Corvera and Antonio Moreno, O.F.M. P. Corvera was missionary at San Ildefonso; P. Moreno from Nambe had come to visit him. During the night, the Tehua Indians closed up every window and opening of their cell, then set fire to the convent and the church, leaving the Religious to die suffocated by the smoke and heat.

The Ninth of June.

At Rome, on Mount Cælius, the birthday of the holy martyrs Primus and Felician, under the emperors Diocletian and Maximian. These glorious martyrs lived long in the service of the Lord, and endured sometimes together, sometimes separately, various cruel torments. They were finally beheaded by Promotus, governor of Nomentum, and thus happily ended their combat. — The birthday of St. Ephrem deacon and doctor of the Church, who is honored by many on this day and by others on the 18th of June. — At Iona in Scotland, St. Columba, abbot and confessor.

The Tenth of June.

In Scotland, St. Margaret, queen, celebrated for her love of the poor and of voluntary poverty. Her feast was transferred to her birthday on the 16th of November by Pope Paul VI.

The Eleventh of June.

The birthday of the apostle St. Barnabas, born in Cyprus. By the disciples, he was ordained apostle of the Gentiles with St. Paul, and with him traversed many regions, fulfilling his commission to preach the Gospel. At length he went to Cyprus, where he ennobled his apostolate by a glorious martyrdom. Through his own relevation his body was found, in the time of the emperor Zeno, together with a copy of St. Matthew's gospel copied with his own hand.

The Twelfth of June.

At Salamanca, in Spain, St. John of St. Facundus, confessor, of the Order of Augustinians, renowned for his zeal for the faith, for holiness of life, and miracles. — At Rome, on the Aurelian road, during the persecution of Decius and under the prefect Aurelius, the birthday of the holy martyrs Basilides, Cyrinus, Nabor, and Nazarius, soldiers, who were cast into prison for the confession of the Christian name, scourged with scorpions, and finally decapitated. +

Among those with the reputation of martyrdom, on the coast of Florida, south of Tampa Bay, Father Diego de Peñalosa, O.P. He had come to Florida with Fathers Cancer, Beteta and Garcia. The vessel missed the Bay of Tampa; after searching for it a few days and landing from time to time the Fathers, at last, went ashore a few days before Pentecost and conferred with the natives. Whilst Father Cancer continued the journey towards the Bay, Father Diego with Fuentes, a pious Spaniard, and an Indian woman who had acted as interpreter, remained on shore. But the woman betrayed them and the missionary was killed as well as the layman "with all kinds of ceremony and addresses."

The Thirteenth of June.

At Padua, St. Anthony, a native of Portugal, confessor of the Order of Minorites, illustrious for the sanctity of his life, his miracles, and his preaching.

The Fourteenth of June.

At Cæsarea, in Cappadocia, the consecration of St. Basil, bishop and doctor of the Church, who was eminent for learning and wisdom in the time of the emperor Valens. Being adorned with every virtue, he was a great light in the Church, and defended her with admirable constancy against the Arians and Macedonians.

The Fifteenth of June.

In Basilicata, Italy, near the river Silaro, the birthday of the holy martyrs Vitus, Modestus, and Crescentia, who were brought thither from Sicily, in the reign of Diocletion, and after being plunged into a vessel of melted lead, after being exposed to the beasts, and on the pillory, from which torments they escaped uninjured through the power of God, they ended their religious combats. ✠ *Among those with the reputation of sanctity, at Bloomingdale, Ohio, the Servant of God, Gwen Coniker,* co-founder of the Apostolate of Family Consecration and Catholic Familyland. Her cause was initiated by Bishop Daniel Conlon of Steubenville, Ohio.

The Sixteenth of June.

At Dover, in England, St. Richard, bishop of Chichester, celebrated for holiness and glorious miracles.

The Seventeenth of June.

At Padua, Italy, the birthday of St. Gregory Barbarigo, bishop of that city, who was enrolled in the catalogue of the saints by Pope John XXIII.

The Eighteenth of June.

St. Ephrem, deacon of the church of Edessa, in the time of the emperor Valens. After suffering many trials for the faith of Christ and gaining great renown for holiness and learning, he went to rest in the Lord. — At Rome, on the Ardeatine road, in the persecution of Diocletian, the birthday of the saintly brothers Mark and Marcellian, martyrs, who were arrested by the judge Fabian, tied to a stake, and had sharp nails driven in their feet. As they ceased not to praise the name of Christ, they were pierced through the sides with lances, and thus went to the kingdom of heaven with the glory of martyrdom.

The Nineteenth of June.

At Florence, St. Juliana Falconieri, virgin, foundress of the Sisters of the Order of the Servants of the Blessed Virgin Mary, who was placed among the holy virgins by the Sovereign Pontiff, Clement XII. — At Milan, the holy martyrs Gervase and Protase, brothers. The former, by order of the judge Astasius, was so long scourged with leaded whips, that he expired. The latter, after being scourged with rods, was beheaded. Through divine revelation their bodies were found by St. Ambrose. They were partly covered with blood, and as free from corruption as if they had been put to death that very day. When the translation took place, a blind man recovered his sight by touching their relics, and many persons possessed by demons were delivered. — At Ravenna, the birthday of St. Romuald, abbot, founder of the monks of Camaldoli, who restored and greatly extended monastic discipline, which was much relaxed in Italy. He is honored by many on this day, and by others on the 7th of February.

The Twentieth of June.

The birthday of St. Silverius, pope and martyr. For refusing to reinstate the heretical bishop Anthimus, deposed by his predecessor Agapitus, he was banished to the isle of Pontia, by Belisarius, at the instigation of the wicked empress Theodora, and, consumed by many tribulations for the Catholic faith, he expired. — At Verulam, in England, in the time of Diocletian, St. Alban, martyr, who gave himself up to save a cleric whom he had harbored. After being scourged and subjected to bitter torments, he was sentenced to capital punishment. With him suffered also one of the soldiers that led him to execution, who was converted to Christ on the way, and merited to be baptized in his own blood.

The Twenty-first of June.

At Rome, St. Aloysius Gonzaga, of the Society of Jesus, most renowned for his contempt of the princely dignity, and the innocence of his life. ✝ *Among those with the reputation of martyrdom, at Detroit, Michigan, the Recollect Father Nicholas Bernardin Constantin Delhalle, the first pastor of the first French town in the West. He arrived in Canada from France and was assigned to the pastoral work at Longeuil and St. François de Sales and served as chaplain to the troops. In consequence of the peculiar policy of Cadillac, hostilities broke out between the French and the Ottawas. As Father Delhalle, anxious to put an end to the slaughter, was entering the Fort, some Miamis joined him and the Ottawas opened fire on them. A ball struck Father Delhalle and he fell dead on the spot. He was interred in the church of St. Anne.*

The Twenty-second of June.

At London, in England, the birthday of St. John Fisher, bishop of Rochester and martyr, renowned for his uprightness of life and greatness of soul. For opposing the divorce of King Henry VIII, he was beheaded and his head displayed on a pole, after which it was cast into the Thames. — Also at London, the memory of St. Thomas More, chancellor of the same King, who was beheaded by him on the 6th of July. His commemoration was set by Pope Pius XI for this day, with St. John Fisher. — At Nola, in Campania, the birthday of blessed Paulinus, bishop and confessor, who, although a most noble and wealthy man, made himself poor and humble for Christ; and what is still more admirable, became a slave to liberate a widow's son, who had been carried to Africa by the Vandals, when they devastated Campania. He was celebrated, not only for his learning and exceptional holiness of life, but also for his power over the demons. His great merit has been extolled by Saints Ambrose, Jerome, Augustine and Gregory, in their writings. His body, at first transferred to Benevento, and thence to Rome, was restored to Nola by order of Pius X.

The Twenty-third of June.

The vigil of St. John the Baptist. — In England, St. Hilda, abbess of Whitby. — At Ely, in the same country, St. Ethelreda, queen and virgin, who departed for heaven with a great renown for sanctity and miracles. Her body was found without corruption eleven years afterwards. — Also in England St. Mildred, abbess of Minster-in-Thanet. Her remains were translated to Canterbury in 1030. — In some places, Paulinus of Nola, bishop, who is elsewhere honored on the previous day.

The Twenty-fourth of June.

The Nativity of St. John the Baptist, precursor of our Lord, son of Zachary and Elizabeth, who, while yet in his mother's womb, was filled with the Holy Ghost. ✠ *Among those with the reputation of sanctity, at Pembroke, Massachusetts, the birthday of the Servant of God Father Joseph Múzquiz, priest, who established The Prelature of the Holy Cross and Opus Dei in the United States.*

The Twenty-fifth of June.

In the territory of Guletto, near Nusco, Italy, St. William, confessor, founder of the hermits of Mount Vergine.

The Twenty-sixth of June.

At Rome, on Mount Cœlius, the holy martyrs John and Paul, brothers. The former was steward, the other secretary of the virgin Constantia, daughter of the emperor Constantine. Afterwards, under Julian the Apostate, they received the palm of martyrdom by being beheaded. ✚ *Among those with the reputation of martyrdom, at Tampa Bay, Florida, Father Luis Cancer de Barbastro, O.P. He was a native of Saragossa, Spain, and came to America as superior of a band of Dominican missionaries, working amongst the Indians of Vera Paz, in Central America. He sailed to Florida with fellow priests Diego de Peñalosa, Gregorio de Beteta and Juan Garcia. Father Diego was killed somewhere south of the Bay of Tampa, by the Calusas. Still Father Cancer, having found the bay itself, resolved to remain and preach to the Indians with the other Fathers. When near the shore, he sprang out and, not heeding the remonstrances of his friends, proceeded up the steep bank. A crowd soon gathered and a heavy blow of a club stretched him lifeless on the shore. In an instant the tribe had covered him with*

mortal wounds and rushing to the water's edge drove back the rest with a shower of arrows. — At Vincennes, Indiana, the Servant of God Bishop Simon William Gabriel Bruté de Remur, the first bishop of Vincennes. His cause was opened by Archbishop Daniel M. Buechlein of Indianapolis.

The Twenty-seventh of June.

At Alexandria, in Egypt, the feast of St. Cyril, bishop and doctor of the church, a most celebrated defender of the Catholic faith, who rested in peace with a great reputation of learning and sanctity. In many places he is commemorated on this day, in others on the 9th of February.

The Twenty-eighth of June.

The vigil of the holy apostles Peter and Paul. — At Lyons, in France, the birthday of St. Irenæus, bishop and martyr, who, as is related by St. Jerome, was the disciple of blessed Polycarp, bishop of Smyrna, and lived near the time of the Apostles. After having strenuously opposed the heretics by speech and writing, he was crowned with a glorious martyrdom, with almost all the people of his city, during the persecution of Severus. ✝ *Among those with the reputation of martyrdom, at Aguatuvi, Arizona, Father Francisco de Pottos, O.F.M., the protomartyr of Arizona. Born at Villanueva de los Infantes in Spain, he received the habit of St. Francis at the convent of San Francisco at Mexico. Leaving the motherhouse together with P. Andres Gutierrez and Brother Cristoval de la Concepcion, they founded the mission of San Bernardo amongst the Moquis; in a few years they converted 800 Indians. P. Ponas was poisoned by the medicine men and died at Aguatuvi in the arms of P. Francisco de San Buenaventura. Probably also P. Andres and the Brother were killed.*

The Twenty-ninth of June.

At Rome, the birthday of the holy apostles Peter and Paul, who suffered martyrdom on the same day, under the emperor Nero. Within the city the former was crucified with his head downwards, and buried in the Vatican, near the Triumphal way, where he is venerated by the whole world. The latter was put to the sword and buried on the Ostian way, where he receives similar honors.

The Thirtieth of June.

The commemoration of the holy apostle Paul. — In many places, the festival of the protomartyrs of Rome, who earned their reward under the persecution of Nero. ✝ *Among those with the reputation of sanctity, at New York, New York, the memory of Venerable Pierre Toussaint. He was born in Haiti as a slave and was taken to New York, where he married and became a successful*

hairdresser. He used his earnings for purchasing freedom for other slaves as well as numerous charitable causes in New York both public and private, including housing, educating, and training orphaned children. Pope John Paul II declared his virtues heroic.

Our Lady of Mount Carmel

St. Anne

Precious Blood

St. James

St. Ignatius Loyola

July

The First of July.

In Monterey, California, the memory of St. Junipero Serra, O.F.M., the Apostle of California. Accompanying Portola's land expedition to Upper California, he founded nine California missions which accomplished the conversion of all the natives on the coast as far as Sonoma to the north. Besides extraordinary fortitude, his most conspicuous virtues were insatiable zeal, love of mortification, self-denial and absolute confidence in God. He went to his rest on August 28 and was raised to the altars by Pope Francis. — In some places, the Feast of the Most Precious Blood of Our Lord Jesus Christ.

The Second of July.

In some places, the Visitation of the Blessed Virgin Mary to Elizabeth.

The Third of July.

At Lyons, in France, St. Irenæus, bishop and martyr, who in some places is commemorated on this day. His birthday falls on the 28th of June. — In

Saint Junípero Serra

many places, the feast of the blessed apostle Thomas, who preached the Gospel to the Parthians, the Medes, the Persians and Hyrcanians, who is elsewhere honored on the 21st of December. ✝ *Among those with the reputation of sanctity, at Gulu, Uganda, the Servant of God Brother Norbert McAuliffe S.C., religious, educator and missionary known as the "Holy Man of Gulu". The Vatican decreed the validity of his cause on June 9, 1995.*

The Fourth of July.

Independence Day. In many parishes the Prayer for Government of Archbishop John Carroll is read. In some places is said a proper Mass, in white vestments. — At Teanaostaiaë, near Hillsdale in Ontario, the birthday of St. Antoine Daniel, martyr. The Iroquois having invaded the homeland of the Hurons, among whom he had charge of a mission, he ventured forth from the chapel to meet the enemy alone. He was then pierced with musket balls and arrows, and his body thrown into the flames. The Church keeps his memory together with his companions on the 26th of September or the 19th of October.

The Fifth of July.

At Cremona, Italy, St. Anthony Mary Zaccaria, confessor, founder of the Barnabites and the

Angelic Virgins. Distinguished for all the virtues and for miracles, he was placed among the saints by Leo XIII. His body is venerated in the church of St. Barnabas, at Milan. — At Estremoz, Portugal, the birthday of St. Elizabeth, queen. She is honored in many places on this day, in others on the 8th of July.

✝ *Among those with the reputation of sanctity, at San Juan, Puerto Rico, the Servant of God Rafael Cordero (1790-1868), who founded a school for poor children. His cause was opened in May of 2004.*

The Sixth of July.

At London, in England, the passion of St. Thomas More, who is commemorated on the 22nd of June with St. John Fisher. — At Nettuno, Italy, the birthday of St. Maria Goretti, virgin and martyr. She was enrolled in the catalog of the saints by Pope Pius XII.

The Seventh of July

In Moravia, the saintly bishops Cyril and Methodius, who brought to the faith of Christ many nations in those regions with their kings. Leo XIII prescribed that their feast should be celebrated on the seventh of July, which Paul VI moved to the fourteenth of February.

The Eighth of July.

St. Elizabeth, widow, queen of Portugal. Being renowned for virtues and miracles, she was numbered among the saints by Urban VIII.

The Ninth of July.

At various places in China, the memory of Augustine Zhao Rong and his 119 companions, martyrs. They were enrolled in the catalog of saints by Pope John Paul II. — In some churches, the feast of Our Lady of the Atonement. ✝ *Among those with the reputation of sanctity, at Hawthorne, New York, the Servant of God Mother Mary Alphonsa O.P., foundress of the Dominican Sisters of Hawthorne for the care of cancer patients. Her cause was opened by Edward Cardinal Egan. — At Chicago, Illinois, the Servant of God Father Augustus Tolton, priest, a former slave who became the first black priest and established parishes for African Americans including St. Monica, Chicago. His cause was opened by Cardinal Francis George.*

The Tenth of July.

At Rome, the martyrdom of the seven holy brothers, sons of the saintly martyr Felicitas, namely, Januarius, Felix, Philip, Sylvanus, Alexander, Vitalis, and Martial, in the time of the emperor Antoninus, under Publius, prefect of the city. Januarius, after being scourged with rods and detained in prison, died under the blows inflicted with leaded whips. Felix and Philip were scourged to death. Sylvanus was thrown headlong from an eminence. Alexander, Vitalus, and Martial were condemned to capital punishment. — Also, at Rome, in the persecution of Valerian and Gallienus, the holy virgins and martyrs Rufina and Secunda, sisters, who, after being subjected to torments, the one having her head split open, the other being decapitated, departed for heaven. Their bodies are kept with due honor in the Lateran Basilica, near the baptistery.

The Eleventh of July.

At Rome, the blessed Pius, pope and martyr, who was crowned with martyrdom in the persecution of Marcus Aurelius Antoninus. — In many places, the memory of St. Benedict, abbot of Monte Cassino. His birthday is on the 21st of March.

The Twelfth of July.

In the monastery of Passignano, near Florence, the abbot St. John Gualbert, founder of the Vallumbrosan Order.

The Thirteenth of July.

At Göttingen, in Germany, the birthday of St. Henry II, emperor, who kept perpetual chastity with his wife Cunegunde, and induced St. Stephen, king of Hungary, with nearly all his kingdom, to receive the faith of Christ. In many places, he is honored on this day, in others on the 15th of this month.— At Rio Piedras, Puerto Rico, Blessed Carlos Manuel Rodríguez Santiago. He was born November 22, 1918 in Caguas, Puerto Rico, and from an early age took an interest in the liturgy. He translated, edited and published numerous liturgical works, organized a chorus, and worked to spread devotion to the sacred liturgy and particularly the Paschal Vigil. Pope John Paul II beatified him, and his memory is kept on May 4 in Puerto Rico.

The Fourteenth of July.

At Caughnawaga, Canada, the memory of Saint Kateri Tekakwitha, Virgin, the "Lily of the

St. Kateri Tekakwitha

Mohawks." She was born at Ossernenon, New York, in 1656, of a Christian Algonquin mother and a pagan Iroquois father. She was instructed in the faith by Fathers Fremin, Bruyas and Pierron, S. J., and when the clan moved to the northern bank of the Mohawk, near the present town of Fonda, she was baptized by Father Jacques de Lamberville. Thenceforth she practiced her religion unflinchingly in the face of almost unbearable opposition, till finally she was assisted by some Christian Indians to escape to Caughnawaga on the St. Lawrence. Here she lived in the cabin of Anastasia Tegonhatsihonga, a Christian, her sanctity impressing not only her own people but also the French and the missionaries. Her mortifications were extreme. She died April 17th and was raised to the altars by Pope Benedict XVI. — At Lyons, in France, St. Bonaventure, Cardinal and bishop of Albano, confessor and doctor of the Order of Minorites, most celebrated for his learning and holiness of life. His birthday is on the 15th of this month.— At Rome, the birthday of St. Camillus de Lellis. He is honored in some places on the 18th of July.

The Fifteenth of July.

In some places, the memory of St. Henry II, emperor. In many places, he is honored on his birthday on the 13th of this month. — The birthday of St. Bonaventure, bishop. He is honored by many on this day, and by others on the 14th of this month.

The Sixteenth of July.

The festival of the Blessed Virgin Mary of Mount Carmel.

The Seventeenth of July.

At Rome, St. Alexius, confessor, son of the senator Euphemian. Leaving his spouse untouched the night of his marriage, he withdrew from his house, and after a long pilgrimage returned to Rome, where he was seventeen years harbored in his father's house as an unknown beggar, thus deluding the world by a new device. But after his death, becoming known through a voice heard in the churches of the city, and by his own writing, he was, under the Sovereign Pontiff, Innocent I, translated to the church of St. Boniface, where he wrought many miracles. + *Among those with the reputation of martyrdom, at Purisima Concepcion (Fort Yuma, California), the Franciscan Fathers Francisco Hermenegildo Garcés and Juan Barreneche, Martyrs. Father Garcés, a famous explorer and missionary, had been superior at S. Xavier del Bac, Arizona. He was the first Spaniard to penetrate to the Mojave Indians in long journeys through the wilderness and was massacred with the youthful Father Juan Barreneche and others at Purisima Concepcion, a new mission, by the Yuma Indians.—On the same day at San Pedro y Pablo de Biscuna in California, the memory of the Franciscan Fathers Juan Diaz and Matias Moreno, Martyrs. When Father*

Garces undertook the establishment of a regular mission amongst the Yumas, these two fathers accompanied him to the mouth of the Gila and were appointed to the new pueblo of San Pedro y Pablo, eight miles southwest of Concepcion. They were killed by the Yumas on the same day with Father Garces.

The Eighteenth of July.

The feast of St. Camillus de Lellis, confessor, founder of the Clerks Regular ministering to the sick, whose birthday is the 14th of July. Leo XIII declared him Celestial Patron of hospitals and the infirm. — At Tivoli, Italy, in the time of the emperor Hadrian, St. Symphorosa, wife of the martyr St. Getulius, with her seven sons, Crescens, Julian, Nemesius, Primitivus, Justinus, Stacteus, and Eugenius. Their mother, because of her invincible constancy, was first buffeted a long time, then suspended by her hair, and lastly thrown into the river with a stone tied to her body. Her sons had their limbs distended by pulleys and bound to stakes, and terminated their martyrdom by different kids of death. The bodies were subsequently taken to Rome, and were found in the sacristy of St. Angelo in Piscina, under the Sovereign Pontiff, Pius IV.

The Nineteenth of July.

St. Vincent de Paul, confessor, who slept in the Lord on the 27th of September. Leo XIII declared him heavenly patron before the throne of God of all charitable organizations throughout the Catholic world owing in any manner their origin to him.

The Twentieth of July.

In some places, the feast of St. Jerome Emiliani, confessor, whose birthday is February 8th. — At Antioch, St. Margaret, virgin and martyr. — At Ravenna, the bishop St. Apollinaris. — At Barcelona, Spain, the birthday of Blessed Father Lucas Tristany OCD, martyr, who served as a priest of the Tucson diocese. His memory is kept on November 6th. ✝ *Among those with the reputation of martyrdom, near the Rio Grande in Texas the memory of Father Silva, O.F.M. Father Silva worked amongst the Apaches but the friendly intercourse between the Franciscans and the Apaches, aroused hostile feelings among the Texas tribes in the missions, who regarded the Apaches as their natural enemies. Therefore a party of mission Indians killed him.*

The Twenty-first of July.

At Lisbon, St. Lawrence of Brindisi, confessor, superior general of the Capuchin Minorites of St. Francis. Illustrious by his preaching and his arduous labor for the glory of God, he was canonized by Leo XIII. — At Rome, the holy virgin Praxedes, who was brought up in all chastity and in the knowledge of the divine law. Assiduously attending to watching, prayer and fasting, she rested in Christ, and was buried near her sister Pudentiana, on the Salarian Road.

The Twenty-second of July.

At Marseilles, France, the birthday of St. Mary Magdalen, out of whom our Lord expelled seven demons, and who deserved to be the first to see the Savior after He had risen from the dead.

The Twenty-third of July.

The birthday of the holy bishop Apollinaris, who was consecrated at Rome by the Apostle Peter, and sent to Ravenna, where he endured for the faith of Christ many different tribulations. He afterwards preached the Gospel in Æmilia, where he converted many from the worship of idols. Finally, returning to Ravenna, he terminated his confession of Christ by a glorious martyrdom under the Cæsar Vespasian. — At Le Mans, in France, St. Liborius, bishop and confessor. — At Rome, the birthday of St. Bridget, widow. In many places she is honored on this day, in others on the 8th of October.

The Twenty-fourth of July.

At Tyro, in Tuscany, on Lake Bolsena, St. Christina, virgin and martyr. Believing in Christ, and breaking up her father's gold and silver idols to give them to the poor, she was cruelly scourged by his command, subjected to other most severe torments, and thrown with a heavy stone into the lake, from which she was drawn out by an angel. Then under another judge, who succeeded her father, she bore courageously still more bitter tortures. Finally, after she had been shut up by the governor Julian in a burning furnace for five days without any injury, and after being cured of the sting of serpents, she ended her martyrdom by having her tongue cut out, and being pierced with arrows. — At Annaya, in Lebanon, the memory of St. Charbel Makhluf, priest, who was enrolled in the catalog of the saints by Pope Paul VI.

The Twenty-fifth of July.

St. James the Apostle, brother of the blessed evangelist John, who was beheaded by Herod Agrippa about the feast of Easter. His sacred bones were on this day carried from Jerusalem to Spain, and placed in the remote province of Galicia, where they are devoutly honored by the far-famed piety of the inhabitants, and the frequent concourse of Christians, who visit them through piety and in fulfillment of their vows. — At Moncada, Spain, the birthday of Blessed Father Eduardo Farré, OCD, martyr, who served as a priest of the Tuscon diocese in Arizona. His memory is kept on November 6. — In Lycia, in the time of Decius, St. Christopher, martyr. Being scourged with iron rods, cast into the flames, from which he was saved by the power of Christ, and finally transfixed with arrows and beheaded, he completed his martyrdom.

The Twenty-sixth of July.

The departure out of this life of St. Anne, mother of the Blessed Virgin Mary, Mother of God. — Also in many churches, St. Joachim, father of the Blessed Virgin Mary.

The Twenty-seventh of July.

At Nicomedia, the martyrdom of St. Pantaleon, a physician. For the faith of Christ he was apprehended by the emperor Maximian, subjected to the torture and burned with torches, during which torments he was comforted by an apparition of our Lord. He ended his martyrdom by a stroke of the sword.

The Twenty-eighth of July.

At Milan, the birthday of the holy martyrs Nazarius and a boy named Celsus. While the persecution excited by Nero was raging, they were beheaded by Anolinus, after long sufferings and afflictions endured in prison. — At Rome, the martyrdom of St. Victor, pope and martyr. — Also at Rome, St. Innocent, pope and confessor. ✝ *Among those with the reputation of martyrdom, at Santiago Atitlán, Guatemala, Father Stanley Rother, priest and missionary from the Diocese of Oklahoma City who translated the Gospels into Tzutihil, he was shot in the head by gunmen who had broken into his rectory.*

The Twenty-ninth of July.

At Tarascon, in France, St. Martha, virgin, the hostess of our Savior, and sister of blessed Mary Magdalen and St. Lazarus. — At Rome, on the Aurelian road, St. Felix II, pope and martyr. Being expelled from his See by the Arian emperor Constantius for defending the Catholic faith, and being put to the sword privately at Cera, in Tuscany, he died gloriously. ✝ *Among those with the reputation of sanctity, at Lackawanna, New York, Venerable Father Nelson Baker. He served in the Civil War and was a decade later ordained a priest. Founder of the Association of Our Lady of Victory, he oversaw the building of the minor basilica of that name as well as a "city of charity" consisting of numerous charitable institutions. Pope Benedict XVI declared his virtues heroic.*

The Thirtieth of July.

At Rome, in the reign of Decius, the holy Persian martyrs Abdon and Sennen, who were bound with chains, brought to Rome, scourged with leaded whips for the faith of Christ, and then put to the sword. — At Imola, in Italy, the birthday of St. Peter Chrysologus, bishop of Ravenna, celebrated for his learning and sanctity.

The Thirty-first of July.

At Rome, the birthday of St. Ignatius, confessor, founder of the Society of Jesus, renowned for sanctity and miracles, and most zealous for propagating the Catholic religion in all parts of the world. ✠ *Among those with the reputation of sanctity, at Detroit, Michigan the Venerable Father Solanus Casey O.F.M. Cap. Born in Oak Grove, Wisconsin, he joined the Order of Friars Minor Capuchin and served as a friary porter in New York, Detroit, and Huntington Indiana, where he became renowned for his compassion, words of comfort, and good counsel as well as his personal holiness. Pope John Paul II declared his virtues heroic.*

Transfiguration

Decollation of John the Baptist

Assumption

St. Clare

St. Augustine

August

The First of August.

At Antioch, the martyrdom of the seven holy brothers, the Machabees, and their mother, who suffered under king Antiochus Epiphanes. Their relics were transferred to Rome, and placed in the church of St. Peter, just mentioned. — The birthday of St. Alphonse Maria de Liguori. In many places he is honored on this day, in others on the day following.

The Second of August.

At Nocera-de-Pagani, St. Alphonse Maria de Liguori, bishop of St. Agatha of the Goths, and founder of the Congregation of the Most Holy Redeemer, distinguished by his zeal for the salvation of souls, by his writings, his preaching, and his example. He was inscribed on the calendar of the saints by Pope Gregory XVI, in the year 1839, the fifty-second year after his happy death, and was declared Doctor of the Universal Church by Pius IX, according to a decree of the Sacred Congregation of Rites. — At Rome, in the cemetery of Callistus, the birthday of St. Stephen, pope and martyr. In the persecution of Valerian, the soldiers suddenly entered whilst he was saying Mass, but he remained before the altar and concluded the sacred mysteries with intrepidity, and was beheaded on his throne. — St. Eusebius of Vercelli, bishop and martyr, whose birthday is on the 1st of this month. He is honored in some places on the 16th of December. — At La Mure d'Isère, in France, St. Peter Julian Eymard, priest, founder of the Society of the Blessed Sacrament and of the Servants of the Blessed Sacrament.

The Fourth of August.

At Bologna, St. Dominic, confessor, founder of the Order of Friars Preachers, most renowned for sanctity and learning. He preserved his chastity unsullied to the end of his life, and by his great merits raised three persons from the dead. After having repressed heresies by his preaching, and instructed many in the religious and godly life, he rested in peace on the 6th of this month. His feast celebrated on this day by decree of Pope Paul IV and on the 8th of this month by decree of Pope Paul VI. — The birthday of St. John Mary Vianney, priest and confessor. He is honored by many on this day, and by some on the 8th of this month.

The Fifth of August.

At Rome, on Mount Esquiline, the dedication of the basilica of St. Mary Major, also called St. Mary of the Snows.

The Sixth of August.

On Mount Tabor, the transfiguration of our Lord Jesus Christ. — At Rome, on the Appian road, in the cemetery of Callistus, the birthday of blessed Sixtus II, pope and martyr, who received the crown of martyrdom in the persecution of Valerian, by being put to the sword. ✝ *Among those with the reputation of sanctity, in the city of Mexico the venerable servant of God, Father Antonio Margil, O.F.M., the Apostle of Texas. He led a band of three fathers and two lay brothers into Texas and founded the missions of Guadalupe among the Nacogdoches, Dolores amongst the Ays, and San Miguel amongst the Adays. When the French destroyed these missions, Father Margil withdrew to the Rio San Antonio and remained near the present city of San Antonio for more than a year.*

He then returned with his friars to the scene of his former activities, restored the missions and even gave his attention to the French settlers in Louisiana. Later on he resumed missionary work in Mexico. He died at the convent of San Francisco, in the odor of sanctity. Pope Gregory XVI declared Father Margil's virtues heroic.

The Seventh of August.

At Naples, in Campania, St. Cajetan of Tiene, confessor, founder of the Theatines, who, through singular confidence in God, made his disciples practice the primitive mode of life of the Apostles. Being renowned for miracles, he was ranked among the saints by Clement X. — At Arezzo, in Tuscany, the birthday of St. Donatus, bishop and martyr, who among other miraculous deeds, made whole again by his prayers (as is related by the blessed pope Gregory), a sacred chalice which had been broken by pagans. Being apprehended by the imperial officer Quadratian, in the persecution of Julian the Apostate, and refusing to sacrifice to idols, he was struck with the sword, and thus consummated his martyrdom. — In many places the memory of St. Sixtus, pope and martyr, whose birthday is on the previous day. ✝ *Among those with the reputation of martyrdom and sanctity, at Hawikuh (Zuñi) in New Mexico Father Pedro de Avila y Ayala, O.F.M. When the Apache Indians attacked the Zuñi pueblo of Hawikuh, this pious missionary won his crown. — At Long Beach Island, New Jersey, the Servant of God María Esperanza Medrano Parra de Bianchini, Venezuelan mystic and recipient of Marian apparitions and supernatural gifts. Her cause was opened by Bishop Paul Bootkoski of the Diocese of Metuchen.*

The Eighth of August.

At Ars-sur-Formans, France, St. John Mary Vianney, priest and confessor, renowned for his devotion as a parish priest. Pope Pius XI placed him in the number of the saints, and appointed him the heavenly patron of all parish priests. — At Rome, the holy martyrs Cyriacus, deacon, Largus, and Smaragdus, with twenty others, who suffered on the 16th of March, in the persecution of Diocletian and Maximian. Their bodies were buried on the Salarian road by the priest John, but were on this day translated by pope St. Marcellus to the estate of Lucia, on the Ostian way. Afterwards they were brought to Rome, and placed in the Church of St. Mary in Via Lata. — In many places, the memory of St. Dominic, confessor and founder of the Order of Friars Preachers, whose birthday is on the 6th of this month.

The Ninth of August.

The vigil of St. Lawrence, martyr. — At Rome, St. Romanus, soldier, who was moved by the torments of blessed Lawrence to ask for baptism from him. He was immediately prosecuted, scourged, and finally beheaded. — At Kalaupapa, Hawaii, the birthday of St. Mother Marianne Cope, O.S.F. Her memory is kept on January 23. — At Auschwitz, in

Poland, the birthday of St. Theresa Benedicta of the Cross, religious and martyr. She was enrolled in the catalog of the saints by Pope John Paul II. ✝ *Among those with the reputation of martyrdom, near New Orleans, Louisiana, Father Jean Daniel Testu. He was a native of Cape-Saint-Ignace, Canada and went to join Father Francois Jolliet de Martigny in the mission field in the Mississippi Valley. Father Testu founded a mission amongst the Choctaws in Louisiana. On their way to Mobile, he and his party, while cabining at night on the shore, were attacked by Indians. At the first volley Father Testu received a fatal wound.*

The Tenth of August.

At Rome, on the Tiburtine road, the birthday of the blessed archdeacon Lawrence, a martyr during the persecution of Valerian. After much suffering from imprisonment, from scourging with whips set with iron or lead, from hot metal plates, he at last completed his martyrdom by being slowly consumed on an iron instrument made in the form of a gridiron. His body was buried by blessed Hippolytus and the priest Justin in the cemetery of Cyriaca, in the Veran field. — At Assisi, in Italy, the birthday of St. Clare, virgin. Her feast was traditionally observed on the following day but was restored to this day by Pope Paul VI. ✝ *Among those with the reputation of martyrdom, at the Tesuque pueblo, New Mexico, Father Juan Bautista de Pio, O.F.M. He was a native of Victoria, Spain, and was attached to the mission church of Santa Fe,*

New Mexico. He had gone to Tesuque to say Mass, when the revolt of the Tejuan El Popé (Poc-pec) broke out. Father Pio was killed by the Indians, the first victim of the revolution. His Mass server, the soldier Pedro Hidalgo, escaped. —At the Tano pueblo of Santa Cruz de Galisteo, New Mexico, the Franciscan Fathers Juan Bernal and Juan Domingo de Vera. Father Juan was custodio of the missions of New Mexico during the great insurrection. Father Bernal had been warned by the Tanos of San Cristóval and San Lazaro, but the Spanish governor took measures to prevent the revolt, when it was too late. Three hundred and eighty Spaniards, men, women and children, were killed, all the churches and Spanish settlements destroyed and every vestige of Christianity stamped out amongst the Zuñis, Moquis, Navajos, Taos, Picuries and Tejuas. — At the Convent of Porciuncula, amongst the Pecos Indians in New Mexico, Father Fernando de Velasco, O.F.M., the chief of the Pecos, communicated to the authorities the plans of El Popé to exterminate all the Spaniards. Finding his advice unheeded, he told Father Fernando: "Father, the people are going to rise and kill the Spaniards and missionaries. Decide then, whether you wish to go and I will send warriors with you and protect you." Thereupon Father Fernando hurried to warn Father Bernal at Galisteo, but was overtaken by the Indians and shot to death with arrows, at daybreak.— At the Tehua pueblo of Nambe, New Mexico, the Franciscan missionary Father Tomas de Torres. He was a native of Tepozotlan, Mexico. He was also killed at the outbreak of the insurrection of El Popé. — In the pueblo of the Tanos Indians, New Mexico, Father Simon de Jesus, O.F.M. He had served the Tanos for fourscore years. Seeing the talent, intelligence and apparent piety of an Indian boy, Frasquillo, he devoted his time to the education of the youth. When, however, the revolt broke out under El Popé, Frasquillo entered ardently into it and slew with his own hands the priest who had done so much to elevate him. He was then hailed by the Tanos as king. — At the pueblo of San Lorenzo de Picuries, New Mexico, Father Matias de Rendon, O.F.M. He was a native of Puebla de los Angeles, Mexico, and was killed by his own flock during the revolt of El Popé.

The Eleventh of August.

At Rome, between the two laurels situated about three miles from the city, the birthday of St. Tiburtius, martyr, under the judge Fabian, in the persecution of Diocletian. After he had walked barefoot on burning coals and confessed Christ with increased constancy, he was put to the sword. — Also, at Rome, the holy virgin Susanna, a woman of noble race, and niece of the blessed Pontiff Caius. She merited the palm of martyrdom by being beheaded in the time of Diocletian. ✝ *Among those with the reputation of martyrdom, at San Diego de los Jemes, New Mexico, the Franciscan missionary Juan de Jesus. He was a native of Granada, Spain. He had worked amongst his people for nine years, when the Indian revolt of El Popé broke out. P. Juan was stripped, tied on a hog and chased through the pueblo amid the curses and blows of the rabble. Then they sat upon him and made him carry them around on all fours, until he sank lifeless, on August 11, 1680. His relics were taken, August 8, 1694, by Governor de Vargas, and deposited in the church of San Francisco at Santa Fe, August 11, 1694.—At the Indian pueblo San Esteban de Acoma in New Mexico the memory of Father Lucas Maldonado, O.F.M. Martyr. He was killed by his*

Indians during the revolt of El Popé, August, 1680. He was a native of Tribugena, Spain, and held the office of Definidor aĉtual.— At the pueblo Purisima Concepcion de Alona, New Mexico, the memory of Father Juan de Val, O.F.M. He was a native of Castile, Spain. After having worked at Alona for nine years, he was killed by the Zuñi Indians, during the insurreĉtion of El Popé. —At the pueblo of San Geronimo de Taos, New Mexico, the memory of Father Antonio Mora and the lay brother Juan de Pedrosa, O.F.M. Father Mora had been in service amongst the Taos for nine years. He was a native of Puebla de los Angeles, Mexico. Brother de Pedrosa was born in Mexico City. They gave their lives for Christ during the insurreĉtion of the Indian El Popé against the Spaniards, in August, 1680. —At the Indian pueblo of San Ildefonso, New Mexico, the memory of Father Luis de Morales, O.F.M., and the lay brothers Antonio Sanchez de Pró and Luis de Baeza. Father Morales was born at Ubeda, Spain Brother de Pró was a native of Mexico City; he had joined the Discalced Carmelites, but had gone over to the Observants of St. Francis, in order to be able to go to the missions in New Mexico. The three friars were killed at San Ildefonso during the revolt of El Popé.—At San Marcos pueblo, New Mexico, the memory of the Franciscan Father Manuel de Tinoco. He had joined the Order of St. Francis in the province of San Miguel de Estremadura. He was killed during the Indian revolt of El Popé.

The Twelfth of August.

At Assisi, Italy, St. Clare, virgin, the first of the poor women of the Order of Minorites. Being celebrated for holiness of life and miracles, she was

placed among holy virgins by Alexander IV. —
St. Jane Frances de Chantal, foundress of the Order
of Nuns of the Visitation of St. Mary, whose feast
was transferred to this day by Pope John Paul II. ✝

*Among those with the reputation of martyrdom, at San Bernardo
de Aguatuvi, Arizona, Father José de Figueras, O.F.M. He was
born in the city of Mexico and came to Arizona where he served the
Hopi pueblo of Aguatuvi, 26 miles from the Zuñi pueblos. When
the Indians rose against the Spaniards, he foretold them that within
three years they would be at war with each other. He was killed with
clubs and stones and his body thrown into a cave. — At the pueblo of
San Bartolme de Xongopavi (Xenopoli) in Arizona, Father José de
Trujillo, O.F.M. He worked in the Hopi pueblo of San Bartolme,
seven leagues from Aguatuvi. His own Indians killed him during the
insurrection of El Popé. — At the pueblo of Santo Domingo, New
Mexico, the Franciscan missionaries P. Juan Talaban, Francisco
Antonio de Lorenzana and Juan Montesdoca. Father Talaban had
worked in the missions of New Mexico for twenty years; he had been
custodio of the missions. Father de Lorenzana was born in Galicia,
Spain, P. Montesdoca at Queretaro, Mexico. During the great revolt
of El Popé, the three priests were locked up in their house by the
Indians who set fire to it, thus stifling and burning the friars. — In
the country of the Zuñi Indians, New Mexico, the memory of the
Franciscan Fathers Lorenzo Analisa, Juan Espinosa and Sebastian
Casalda. They were stripped, stoned, and at last shot to death in the
public place. Their bodies were buried in the ruins of the church.*

The Thirteenth of August.

At Rome, blessed Hippolytus, martyr, who gloriously confessed the faith, under the emperor Valerian. After enduring torments, he was tied by the feet to the necks of wild horses, and being cruelly dragged through briars and brambles, and having all his body lacerated, he yielded up his spirit. — The same day, the birthday of St. Pontian, pope and martyr, who with the priest Hippolytus, was transported to Sardinia, by the emperor Alexander, and there, being scourged to death with rods, consummated his martyrdom. His body was conveyed to Rome by the blessed pope Fabian, and buried in the cemetery of Callistus. — At Imola, Italy, the birthday of St. Cassian, martyr. As he refused to worship idols, the persecutor called the boys whom the saint taught and who hated him, giving them leave to kill him. The torment suffered by the martyr was the more grievous, as the hand that inflicted it, by reason of its weakness, rendered death more tardy.

The Fourteenth of August.

The vigil of the Assumption of the blessed Virgin Mary. — At Rome, the birthday of the blessed priest Eusebius, who for the defense of the Catholic faith was shut up in a room of his own house by the Arian emperor Constantius, where constantly persevering in prayer for seven months, he rested in peace. — At Auschwitz, in Poland, the memory of St. Maximilian Kolbe, missionary priest and martyr of charity. ✝ *Among those with the reputation of martyrdom and sanctity, on the Menominee River, in Wisconsin, the Jesuit Father René Menard. He was assigned to work amongst the Hurons. After the destruction of the Huron mission, he was sent to the Cayugas, in the Iroquois country, where, for the first three months, he was brutally treated, but succeeded in gaining the confidence of the Indians. When the Iroquois mission was interrupted, he went to Three Rivers and started with 300 Ottawas for the far west. He reached the shores of Lake Superior and endeavored to establish a mission in Keweenaw, Michigan, whence he set out to visit other tribes. On his way to the Hurons on Noquet Island at the mouth of the Menominee River, he was separated from his companion; he lost his way in the forests and was never heard of again, murdered by a roving band of Sioux, probably at the first rapids of the Menominee,*

near the present city of Crystal Falls. — At Thomaston, Connecticut the birthday of Venerable Father Michael J. McGivney. While a parish priest at St. Mary's Church in New Haven, he founded the Knights of Columbus. He died of pneumonia, his life being declared of heroic virtue by Pope Benedict XVI.

The Fifteenth of August.

THE ASSUMPTION OF THE MOST HOLY VIRGIN MARY, MOTHER OF GOD. ✝ *Among those with the reputation of sanctity, at Cataldo, Idaho, Louise Siuwheem Polotkin of the Coeur d'Alene nation. Daughter of a chief and grandchild of Chief Circling Raven who prophesied the coming of the Black Robes, she was baptized by Father DeSmet. She married Adolph Polotkin and had three sons, serving as a teacher and catechist, zealous for the faith and beloved for her charity. She was called the spiritual director and guardian angel of the nation. Louise died to an enormous outpouring of grief, but the day is unrecorded. The Coeur D'Alene make pilgrimage to the old mission on this day for the Assumption and the memory of their "Good Grandmother", and they have erected there a stone monument in her honor.*

The Sixteenth of August.

St. Joachim, father of the most blessed Virgin Mary, whose birthday is the 20th of March. — At Alba, in Hungary, St. Stephen, king of Hungary, who, being adorned with divine virtues, was the first to convert the Hungarians to the faith of Christ. He was received into heaven by the Virgin Mother of God, on the day of her Assumption. His feast is observed traditionally on the 2nd of September and was transferred to this day by Pope Paul VI.

The Seventeenth of August.

At Cracow, in Poland, St. Hyacinth, confessor, of the Order of Preachers, who slept in the Lord on the 16th of this month.

The Eighteenth of August.

At Palestrina, the birthday of the holy martyr Agapitus. Although only fifteen years of age, as he was fervent in the love of Christ, he was arrested by order of the emperor Aurelian, and scourged a long time. Afterwards, under the prefect Antiochus, he endured more severe torments, and being delivered to the lions by the emperor's order without receiving any injury, he was finally struck with the sword, and thus merited his crown. — The feast of St. John Eudes was formerly celebrated on this day but was transferred to the following day, his birthday, by Pope Paul VI. ✛ *Among those with the reputation of sanctity, at Evansville, Indiana, the Servant of God Mother Mary Magdalen Bentivoglio, O.S.C., foundress of the first monastery of Poor Clares in the United States.*

The Nineteenth of August.

At Caen, France, St. John Eudes, missionary, founder of the Congregation of Priests of Jesus and Mary and of the Congregation of the Sisters of Our Lady of Charity, and promoter of the cult of the most Sacred Hearts of Jesus and Mary. He was canonized by Pope Pius XI.

The Twentieth of August.

In the territory of Langres, France, the demise of St. Bernard, first abbot of Clairvaux, illustrious for virtues, learning, and miracles. He was declared Doctor of the universal church by Sovereign Pontiff, Pius VIII. ✝ *Among those with the reputation of sanctity, at Parma, Italy, Mother Celestina Bottego, native of Glendale, Ohio and foundress of the missionaries of Mary. Her cause has been opened in the diocese of Parma.*

The Twenty-first of August.

At Rome, the memory of St. Pius X, pope, whose birthday is on the previous day. — The festival of St. Jane Frances Fremiot de Chantal, foundress of the Order of Nuns of the Visitation of St. Mary.

The Twenty-second of August.

The feast of the Immaculate Heart of Mary, or the Queenship of the Blessed Virgin Mary. — At Rome, on the Ostian road, the birthday of the holy martyr Timothy. After he had been arrested by Tarquinius, prefect of the city, and kept for a long time in prison, as he refused to sacrifice to the idols, he was scourged three times, subjected to the most severe torments, and finally beheaded. — At Porto, St. Hippolytus, bishop, most renowned for learning.

Having gloriously confessed the faith, in the time of the emperor Aurelian, he was bound hand and foot, precipitated into a deep ditch filled with water, and thus received the palm of martyrdom. — At Autun, St. Symphorian, a martyr, in the time of the emperor Aurelian. Refusing to offer sacrifice to the idols, he was first scourged, then confined in prison, and finally ended his martyrdom by being beheaded.

The Twenty-third of August.

At Todi, St. Philip Benizi of Florence, confessor. He contributed greatly to the growth of the Order of the Servites of the Blessed Virgin Mary, and was a man of the greatest humility. He was numbered among the saints by Clement X. — In many places, the feast of St. Rose of Lima, virgin, whose birthday is on the 26th of this month. + *Among those with the reputation of martyrdom, at Norridgewock Mission, Maine, Father Sebastien Rale (Rasle) S.J. His first missionary work was in an Abenaki village near Quebec; next he labored in the Illinois country for two years. He was then sent to the Abenaki mission on the Kennebec. The colonists of New England regarded with suspicion and hatred the arrival of a Frenchman in the midst of tribes who were hostile to the English. Hence the Indian outrages perpetrated on the eastern frontier of New England during his long residence among the Abenakis were attributed to him, and his church was burned. Rale remained and rebuilt it, but later he, with several chiefs and many of his flock, was killed, scalped and hacked to pieces by the Mohawk allies of the English.*

The Twenty-fourth of August.

The apostle St. Bartholomew, who preached the Gospel of Christ in India. He passed thence into Greater Armenia, where, after converting many to the faith, he was flayed alive by the barbarians, and beheaded by order of king Astyages, and thus he terminated his martyrdom.

The Twenty-fifth of August.

At Paris, St. Louis, confessor, king of France, illustrious by the holiness of his life and the fame of his miracles. — The birthday of St. Joseph Calasanctius. His feast was formerly observed on the 27th of this month, and moved to this day by Pope Paul VI.

The Twenty-sixth of August.

At Rome, St. Zephirinus, pope and martyr.

The Twenty-seventh of August.

At Rome, the demise of St. Joseph Calasanctius, confessor, illustrious by the innocence of his life and miracles, who, to instruct youth in piety and letters, founded the Order of the Poor Clerks

Regular of the pious Schools of the Mother of God. His birthday is on the 25th of this month. — In many places, the memory of St. Monica, whose feast was moved to this day by Pope Paul VI. — At Bamburgh, in England, St. Aidan, bishop of Lindisfarne. When St. Cuthbert, then a shepherd, saw his soul going up to heaven, he left his sheep and became a monk.

The Twenty-eighth of August.

At Hippo Regius, in Africa, the birthday of St. Augustine, bishop and famous doctor of the Church. Converted and baptized by the blessed bishop Ambrose, he defended the Catholic faith with the greatest zeal against the Manichaeans and other heretics, and after having sustained many other labors for the Church of God, he went to his reward in heaven. — In Monterey, the birthday of Saint Junipero Serra, O.F.M., the Apostle of California. His memory is kept on July 1st. — At Rome, the birthday of Hermes, an illustrious man, who was first confined in prison, and afterwards ended his martyrdom by the sword, under the judge Aurelian.

The Twenty-ninth of August.

The beheading of St. John the Baptist, who was put to death by Herod about the feast of Easter. However, the solemn commemoration takes place today, when his venerable head was found for the second time. — At Rome, on Mount Aventine, the birthday of St. Sabina, martyr. Under the emperor Hadrian, she was struck with the sword, and thus obtained the palm of martyrdom.

The Thirtieth of August.

The feast of St. Rose of Lima, virgin, whose birthday is on the 26th of this month. — At Rome, on the Ostian road, the martyrdom of the blessed priest Felix, under the emperors Diocletian and Maximian. After being racked he was sentenced to death, and as they led him to execution, he met a man who spontaneously declared himself a Christian, and was forthwith beheaded with him. The Christians not knowing his name, called him Adauctus, because he was added to St. Felix and shared his crown. — At York, in England, St. Margaret Clitherow, martyr, who was crushed to death by stones for harboring a priest. She entered heaven on the 25th of March. — At Tyburn, in England, St. Anne Line, martyr, who for the same charge was hung by the neck at the

scaffold, on the 27th of February. — Also at Tyburn
St. Margaret Ward, martyr, who for aiding a priest
was suspended by the hands and scourged, after which
she was hung at the scaffold and won her crown on this
day.

The Thirty-first of August.

At Cardona, in Spain, St. Raymond Nonnatus,
cardinal and confessor, of the Order of
Mercedarians, renowned for holiness of life and
miracles. ✝ *Among those with the reputation of martyrdom,
at the Hopi pueblo of San Francisco de Oraibe, in Arizona, the
Franciscan Fathers José de Espeleta and Augustin a S. Maria. Both
were killed during the revolt of El Popé. Before Father Espeleta was
massacred, the Indians kept him as a slave, like a beast of burden, an
object of ridicule for old and young.*

Nativity of the Blessed Virgin

St. Matthew

Exaltation of the Holy Cross

St. Jerome

St. Michael the Archangel

September

The First of September.

In the province of Narbonne, France, St. Giles, abbot and confessor. — At Benevento, Italy, twelve saintly brothers, martyrs.

The Second of September.

At Alba, in Hungary, St. Stephen, king of Hungary, who, being adorned with divine virtues, was the first to convert the Hungarians to the faith of Christ. He was received into heaven by the Virgin Mother of God, on the day of her Assumption. His feast, nevertheless, is commemorated on this day, according to the Constitution of pope Innocent XI, when the strong fortress of Buda was reconquered through the assistance of the holy king, by the brave Christian army.

The Third of September.

At Rome, the memory of Pope St. Pius X, whose birthday is on August 20th. — In many places, the memory of St. Gregory the Great, whose feast was transferred to this day by Pope Paul VI. His birthday is the 12th of March.

The Fourth of September.

St. Cuthbert, bishop of Lindisfarne in England, who from his childhood to his death was renowned for good works and miracles. + *Among those with the reputation of sanctity, at Châu Lâm, Vietnam, the Servant of God Father Vincent Robert Capodanno, M.M. of Staten Island, New York, killed in action ministering to the wounded during the Vietnam War.*

The Fifth of September.

The feast of St. Lawrence Justinian, first patriarch of Venice, who by his glorious miracles and virtues, illustrated the episcopal dignity which he received against his will on this day. His birthday is the 8th of January.

The Eighth of September.

The Nativity of the most Blessed and ever Virgin Mary, Mother of God. — At Nicomedia, Turkey, St. Hadrian, with twenty-three other martyrs, who ended their martyrdom the 4th of March by having their limbs crushed, after enduring many torments under the emperors Diocletian and Maximian. Their remains were carried to Byzantium by the Christians, and buried with due honors. Afterwards the body of St. Hadrian was taken to Rome on this day, on which is festival is celebrated.

The Ninth of September.

At Cartagena, Colombia, St. Peter Claver, confessor of the Society of Jesus, who labored with wonderful self-abnegation and great charity among the negro slaves for more than forty years and baptized personally almost thirty thousand of them. He was canonized by order of Pope Leo XIII. — At Nicomedia, Turkey, the holy martyr Gorgonius. The highest honor had been conferred on him by the emperor Diocletian, but as he and Dorotheus detested the cruelty which he exercised against the Christians, they were by his order suspended in his presence, and lacerated with whips; then their skin being torn from their bodies, and vinegar with salt poured over them, they were burned on a gridiron and finally strangled.

✝ *Among those with the reputation of martyrdom, on the Illinois River the departure of this life of the Recollect Father Gabriel de la Ribourde. He was the last scion of a noble Burgundian house; he renounced the world and its honors to enter the Order of St. Francis, and then, when advanced in years, renounced the comforts of Europe for the wilds of Canada. He came to Quebec and soon became Superior of his Order in the colony. Sent by his successor to Fort Frontenac, near the present city of Kingston, he was assigned as superior to La Salle's party. Later on he remained with Tonti at Fort Crevecoeur, evangelizing the Indians. When Tonti and his party gave up and destroyed the Fort, they set out in a wretched canoe to reach Green Bay. While Tonti and Father Membre, next day, were busy repairing the canoe, Father Gabriel retired apart to say his breviary. While thus engaged, he was met by a party of Kickapoos, out against the Iroquois, who murdered him and threw his body into a hole.*

The Tenth of September.

At Tolentino, Italy, the departure from this life of St. Nicholas of Tolentino, confessor, of the Order of the Augustinians. ✝ *Among those with the reputation of martyrdom, near the Tigua pueblo of Chilili, New Mexico, Father Juan de Santa Maria, O.F.M. When still a young man, he set out for the pueblos of New Mexico, from the Santa Barbara Mines, Chihuahua. With him were Father Francisco Lopez, the superior, and Brother Augustin Ruiz (Rodriguez), the organizer of the expedition. They were protected by eight soldiers under Francisco Chamuscado, and six Mexican Indians. They visited the pueblos of the Piros, Tigua and Queres nations. When the party arrived amongst the Tano Indians at the pueblo of Galisteo, Father Juan became anxious to return to Mexico to render a report, in order that more priests might be sent to the mission. He started alone from the Sandfa mountains, trusting to his knowledge of the stars, but on his way, on the third day, he was killed under a huge stone by a party of roving Indians, near Chilili, Bernalillo Co.*

The Eleventh of September.

At Rome, in the Cemetery of Basilla, on the old Salarian road, the birthday of the holy martyrs Protus and Hyacinth, brothers and eunuchs in the service of blessed Eugenia, who were arrested, in the time of the emperor Gallienus, on the charge o being Christians, and urged to offer sacrifice to the gods. But as they refused, both were most severely scourged, and finally beheaded. ✝ *Among those with the reputation of martyrdom, near Fort Adams, Mississippi, Father Nicolas Foucault, the first martyr of the Seminary of Quebec. He had already accomplished much good amongst the Arkansas, when he set out for Mobile with his servant and two Frenchmen. They took as guides two men of the Koroa tribe, akin to the Arkansas. Led by hopes of plunder, or instigated by hatred, these two murdered the whole party near the Tonica villages. Father Antoine Davion at the time was ascending the Mississippi and discovered on the banks of the river the bodies of these victims of ferocity. He interred them with the rites of the Church.*

The Twelfth of September.

The feast of the most holy Name of the Blessed Virgin Mary, celebrated by order of the Sovereign Pontiff, Innocent XI, on account of the signal victory gained over the Turks, at Vienna in Austria, through her protection. ✝ *Among those with the reputation of sanctity, at Hong Kong, the Servant of God Father Thomas Frederick Price, M.M., priest and co-founder of the Catholic Foreign Mission Society of America, also known as the Maryknoll Fathers and Brothers.*

The Thirteenth of September.

In many churches, the feast of St. John Chrysostom, bishop, who reposed in the Lord on the 14th of this month. He was formerly remembered on the day of the translation of his relics, the 27th of January. ✝ *Among those with the reputation of martyrdom, at St. Augustine, Florida, Pedro de Corpa, O.F.M. He established a neophyte village amongst the Timucua Indians at Tolemato (now the cemetry of St. Augustine), but when he publicly reproved the profligate son of the Cazique who had fled from Guala island to the pagans of Tolomato, he was killed by the young man's partisans whilst kneeling before the altar. His head was severed from the body and set on a spear over the gate.*

The Fourteenth of September.

The Exaltation of the Holy Cross, when the emperor Heraclius, after defeating king Chosroes, brought it back to Jerusalem from Persia. ✝ *Among those with the reputation of martyrdom, at St. Augustine, Florida, Father Juan de Silva O.F.M. He was sent as superior of a band of twelve Franciscan missionaries to work amongst the Timucua and Yamassee tribes on the lower St. John River and the islands on the southern coast of Georgia. He established regular villages of neophytes around St. Augustine, but was killed during the subsequent conspiracy.*

The Fifteenth of September.

The Feast of the Seven Sorrows of the Blessed Virgin Mary. — At Rome, on the Nomentan road, the birthday of St. Nicomedes, priest and martyr. As he said to those who would compel him to sacrifice: "I sacrifice only to the Omnipotent God who reigns in heaven," he was for a long time scourged with leaded whips, and thus went to our Lord. ✝ *Among those with the reputation of martyrdom, on St. Simon's Island, Glynn Co., Georgia, Francisco de Velascola, Franciscan Priest. He formed a village of neophytes at Asao, on St. Simon's Island, Georgia. He was killed by the insurgent Yamassee whilst returning from his church.*

The Sixteenth of September.

The Saints Cornelius and Cyprian, pontiffs and martyrs, whose birthday is on the 14th of this month. — At Chalcedon, Turkey, the birthday of St. Euphemia, virgin and martyr, under the emperor Diocletian and the proconsul Priscus. For faith in our Lord she was subjected to tortures, imprisonment, blows, the torment of the wheel, fire, the crushing weight of stones, the teeth of beasts, scourging with rods, the cutting of sharp saws, burning pans, all of which she survived. But when she was again exposed to the beasts in the amphtitheatre, praying to our Lord to receive her spirit, one of the animals having inflicted a bite on her sacred body, whilst the rest licked her feet, she yielded her unspotted soul to God. ✝ *Among those with the reputation of martyrdom, at Toboqui in Florida, the Franciscan Father Bias Rodriguez. He came to St. Augustine with Father Juan de Silva and established a village of neophytes at Toboqui near St. Augustine. He was killed in the chapel of Our Lady of the Milk after Mass, by the insurgent Yamassee Indians from Tolemato.*

The Seventeenth of September.

The commemoration of the Impression of the Sacred Wounds which St. Francis, founder of the Order of Minorites, received, through a wonderful favor of God, in his hands, feet and side, on Mount Alvernia, in Tuscany. — The birthday of St. Robert Bellarmine, cardinal and doctor of the Church. His feast was formerly kept on the 13th of May and was transferred to this day by Pope Paul VI. ✝ *Among those with the reputation of martyrdom, on Amelia Island, Nassau Co., Florida, the Franciscan Father Miguel de Auñon and the laybrother Antonio de Badajoz. Father Miguel was sent to Florida with Father Juan de Silva, O.F.M. He established himself at Asopo on Amelia Island to the north of St. Augustine and was killed with clubs by the insurgent Yamassee Indians before the altar, together with the laybrother Antonio de Badajoz. Their bodies were later buried at St. Augustine.*

The Eighteenth of September.

At Osimo, Italy, St. Joseph of Cupertino, confessor of the Order of the Minorites Conventual, who was placed among the saints by Clement XIII.

The Nineteenth of September.

At Pozzuoli, Italy, the holy martyrs Januarius, bishop of Benevento, Festus, his deacon, and Desiderius, lector, together with Sosius, deacon of the church of Misenum, Procuus, deacon of Pozzuoli, Eutychius and Acutius, who were bound and imprisoned and then beheaded during the reign of Diocletian. The body of St. Januarius was brought to Naples, and buried in the church with due honors, where even now the blood of the blessed martyr is kept in a vial, and when placed up close to his head, is seen to become liquid and bubble up as it if were just taken from his veins. — At Canterbury, the birthday of the holy bishop Theodore, who was sent to England by pope Vitalian, and was renowned for learning and holiness. — Also the memory of St. Adrian of Canterbury, abbot, a distinguished theologian and scholar, whose birthday is on the 9th of January.

The Twentieth of September.

At Rome, the holy martyrs Eustace and Theopistes, his wife, with their two sons Agapitus and Theophistus. Under the emperor Hadrian, they were condemned to be cast to the beasts, but through the power of God, being uninjured by them, they were shut up in a burning brazen ox, and thus terminated their martyrdom. — At Seoul, in Korea, the memory of Sts. Andrew Kim Taegon, Paul Chong Hasang and companions, martyrs, who endured tortures and won their crowns during various persecutions of the Joseon Dynasty. They were enrolled in the catalog of the saints by Pope John Paul II. ✝ *Among those with the reputation of sanctity, at Chicago, Illinois, the Venerable Mother Mary Theresa Dudzik, O.S.F., Foundress. She was born in Poland and emigrated to Chicago, working and saving her earnings for the benefit of poor neighbors. She founded the Franciscan Sisters of Chicago and opened a home for the aged and an orphanage. Pope John Paul II declared her virtues heroic.*

The Twenty-first of September.

The birthday of St. Matthew, apostle and evangelist, who suffered martyrdom in Ethiopia, while engaged in preaching. The Gospel written by him in Hebrew was, by his own revelation, found in the time of the emperor Zeno, together with the relics of the blessed apostle Barnabas.

The Twenty-second of September.

At Valencia, in Spain, St. Thomas of Villanova, archbishop and confessor, whose birthday is the 8th of September. — At St. Maurice, near Sion, in Switzerland, the birthday of the holy Theban martyrs Maurice, Exuperius, Candidus, Victor, Innocent, and Vitalis, with their companions of the same legion, whose martyrdom for the faith, in the time of Maximian, filled the world with the glory of their sufferings.

The Twenty-third of September.

At Foggia, Italy, the birthday of St. Pio of Pietrelcina, priest, who was renowned in life for holiness of life and of numerous and wonderous miracles. — At Rome, St. Linus, pope and martyr, who governed the Roman church next after the blessed apostle Peter. He was crowned with martyrdom, and buried on the Vatican hill beside the same apostle. — At Iconium, in Turkey, St. Thecla, virgin and martyr, who was converted to the faith by the apostle St. Paul. Under the emperor Nero, she was victorious over the flames and the beasts to which she was exposed for the faith of Christ, and after many combats endured for the instruction of others, she went to Seleucia, where she ended her days in peace.

The Twenty-fourth of September.

The feast of our Lady of Ransom, or in some churches, the feast of Our Lady of Walsingham.

The Twenty-sixth of September.

On this day in some churches is observed the feast of the North American Martyrs, transferred by Pope Paul VI to the 19th of October. — The memory of Cosmas and Damian, martyrs, whose feast was moved to this day by Pope Paul VI. — At Nicomedia, in Turkey, the birthday of the holy martyrs Cyprian and Justina, virgin, under the emperor Diocletian and the governor Eutholmius. Justina suffered much for the faith of Christ and converted Cyprian, who, while a magician, endeavored to bring her under the influence of his magical practices. She afterwards suffered martyrdom with him. Their bodies being exposed to the beasts, were taken away in the night by some Christian sailors, and carried to Rome.

The Twenty-seventh of September.

At Aegea, Syria, during the persecution of Diocletian, the birthday of the holy martyrs Cosmas and Damian, brothers. After miraculously overcoming many torments from bonds, imprisonment, fire, crucifixion, stoning, arrows, and from being cast into the sea, they received capital punishment. — The birthday of St. Vincent de Paul, confessor, whose feast was transferred to this day by Pope Paul VI.

The Twenty-eighth of September.

In Bohemia, St. Wenceslas, duke of Bohemia and martyr, renowned for holiness and miracles. Being murdered in his brother's house, he went triumphantly to heaven. — At Nagasaki, in Japan, St. Lorenzo Ruiz of Manila, martyr, who refused to renounce Christ and was hung upside down in a pit. He earned his crown on the 29th of September. + *Among those with the reputation of martyrdom, on Cumberland Island, Georgia, Father Pedro Martinez, the protomartyr of the Jesuits in the United States. Born in Spain, he was sent to America by S. Francis Borgia. He was a man of great learning, deep humility and fervent zeal. Driven by a storm to the coast of Georgia, he landed with a few companions, but his ship was thrown back to the high sea by the heavy waves. Whilst he tried to reach Florida on foot, he was killed by the natives.*

The Twenty-ninth of September.

On Mount Gargano, in Italy, the commemoration of the blessed archangel Michael. This festival is kept in memory of the day when, under his involution, was consecrated a church, unpretending in its exterior, but endowed with virtue celestial.

Death of Fr. Martinez

— Also in many places the memories of Sts. Gabriel and Raphael, archangels. All three of the angelic feasts were combined on this day by Pope Paul VI. — At Auriesville, in New York, the birthday of St. René Goupil, martyr. Captured with St. Isaac Jogues by the Iroquois, he was brought to the Mohawk town of Ossernenon, where after being beaten and having his nails torn out, he was tomahawked for making the sign of the cross. His feast is celebrated with the other North American martyrs on the 26th of September or on the 19th of October.

The Thirtieth of September.

In Bethlehem of Juda, the decease of St. Jerome, priest and Doctor of the Church, who excelling in all kinds of learning, imitated the life of the most approved monks, and disposed of many monstrous heresies with the sword of his doctrine. Having at length reached a very advanced age, he rested in peace, and was buried hear the manger of our Lord. His body was afterwards conveyed to Rome, and deposited in the basilica of St. Mary the Greater. ✝

Among those with the reputation of martyrdom, at Saint-Sauveur, on Mount Desert Island, Maine, the Jesuit Brother Gilbert Du Thet. The Jesuit Fathers Quentin, Masse and Briard established a peaceful settlement for the conversion of Indians on Soames Sound, Mt. Desert Island. The post was destroyed by the English under Captain Argal of Virginia; Brother Du Thet was killed, the Fathers were carried to Virginia as prisoners.

Guardian Angels

Sts. Simon and Jude

St. Luke

St. Francis

St. Teresa

October

The First of October.

At Rhiems, in France, St. Remigius, bishop and confessor, who converted the Franks to Christ, regenerated Clovis, their king, in the sacred font of baptism and instructed him in the mysteries of the faih. After he had been many years bishop, and had distinguished himself by his sanctity and the power of working miracles, he departed this life on the 13th of January. His festival, however, is kept on this day, when his sacred body was translated. — St. Thérèse of the Child Jesus, virgin of the Order of Discalced Carmelites, special patroness of all missions, and Doctor of the Church. Her birthday is on the 30th of September.

The Second of October

The feast of the holy Guardian Angels.

The Third of October.

At Saint Mary-of-the-Woods, Indiana, the memory of Saint Mother Théodore Guérin S.P., foundress. She was born in France and entered the order of the

Saint Mother Théodore Guérin

Sisters of Providence of Ruillé-du-Loir, taking the name Sister St. Théodore. Bishop Bruté of the diocese of Vincennes, Indiana sent for French religious to attend to the vast charitable needs of the diocese. Her superior recommended Sister Théodore and five other sisters, who were sent to America. There they joined with other postulants and moved into a farmhouse. Sister Théodore was made superior of this new foundation, the Sisters of Providence of Saint Mary-of-the-Woods. There she founded a boarding school for girls, various parish schools, and two orphanages. She was enrolled in the catalog of the saints by Pope Benedict XVI. — In some places, the feast of St. Therese of the Child Jesus, elsewhere honored on October 1st.

The Fourth of October

At Assisi, in Italy, the birthday of St. Francis, confessor, founder of the Order of Minorites, whose life, filled with holy deeds and miracles, was written by St. Bonaventure. — The birthday of Blessed Father Francis Seelos, C.SS.R. His memory is kept on the following day, October 5.

The Fifth of October.

At New Orleans, La., the memory of Blessed Father Francis Seelos, C.SS.R. Born in Bavaria, he entered the Congregation of the Most Holy Redeemer, offering himself for the American mission. He made his profession at Baltimore and was ordained seven months later by Archbishop Eccleston. He was assigned first to Baltimore then to Pittsburgh, where he was made superior. His confessional was constantly besieged by crowds of people of every description. It was said by many that he could read their very souls. His name was proposed for the see of Pittsburgh, but he humbly refused. He served briefly in Detroit and New Orleans, Louisiana, where he went to his rest. He was beatified by Pope John Paul II. — At Messina, in Sicily, the birthday of the holy martyrs Placidus, monk, disciple of the blessed abbot Benedict, and of his brothers Eutychius and Victorinus, and Flavia, virgin, their sister; also of Donatus, Firmatus, deacon, Faustus, and thirty other monks, who were murdered for the faith of Christ by the pirate Manuchas.

The Sixth of October.

At Longueuil, in Canada, the birthday of Blessed Marie-Rose Durocher, foundress of the Sisters of the Holy Names of Jesus and Mary. She was enrolled in the catalog of the blessed by Pope John Paul II. — In Calabria, Italy, St. Bruno, confessor, founder of the Carthusian Order. — At Tumon, Guam, the memory of Blessed Father Diego Luis de San Vitores, S.J., martyr. He was born in Burgos, Spain and was sent as missionary to the Pacific. He founded a mission on Guam, where he and his companion St. Pedro Calungsod ran afoul of the village chief Matapang. When they baptized Matapang's daughter with her mother's permission, the chief became enraged and killed St. Pedro. As Pedro lay dying, Father Diego gave him absolution, then he too was slain. He was beatified by Pope John Paul II. ✠ *Among those with the reputation of sanctity, at New York, New York, the Servant of God, Cardinal Terence James Cooke, Archbishop of New York. His cause has been approved by the Congregation of the Causes of Saints.*

The Seventh of October.

The feast of the Most Holy Rosary of the Blessed Virgin Mary, and the commemoration of Our Lady of Victory, which the sovereign Pontiff, blessed Pius V, on account of the great naval victory gained by the Christians on this day, ordered to be kept annually. — At Rome, on the Ardeatine road, the demise of St. Mark, pope and confessor.

The Eighth of October.

St. Bridget, widow, who, after visiting many holy places by the inspiration of the Holy Spirit, died at Rome on the 23rd of July. Her body was taken to Sweden on the 7th of this month.

The Ninth of October.

At Paris, the birthday of the holy martyrs Denis the Areopagite, bishop, Rusticus, priest, and Eleutherius, deacon. Denis was baptized by the apostle St. Paul, and consecrated first bishop of Athens. Then going to Rome, he was sent to Gaul by the blessed Roman Pontiff Clement, to preach the Gospel. He proceeded to Paris, and after having for some years faithfully filled the office entrusted to him, he was subjected to the severest torments by the prefect Fescenninus, and at length, being beheaded with his companions, completed his martyrdom. — At Rome, St. John Leonardi, confessor, founder of the Congregation of Clerks Regular of the Mother of God. He was illustrious by his labors and miracles, and through his instrumentality missions were established by the Propaganda. — The memory of Blessed John Henry Cardinal Newman, priest, renowned for his writings and defense of the Catholic faith in England. His birthday is on the 11th of August. ✝ *Among those with the reputation of sanctity, at Rome the Servant of God Father Theodore Foley C.P., priest and Superior General of the Passionists.*

The Tenth of October.

At Rome, St. Francis Borgia, Superior General of the Society of Jesus, celebrated for the austerity of his life, the gift of prayer, and for the firmness with which he renounced the dignities of the world, and refused those of the Church.

The Eleventh of October.

In some churches, the feast of the Motherhood of the Blessed Virgin Mary.

The Twelfth of October.

At York, in England, St. Wilfrid, bishop and confessor. ✠ *Among those with the reputation of martyrdom, at the Indian mission of Santa Cruz, California, Father Andrés Quintana, O.F.M. He was a powerful man physically and fearless withal, but full of tenderness and solicitude towards his neophytes. In spite of his charity, he was waylaid and killed by his own mission flock.*

The Thirteenth Day of October.

In England, St. Edward, king, who died on the 5th of January. He is specially honored on this day, on account of the translation of his body.

The Fourteenth Day of October.

At Rome, on the Aurelian road, the birthday of blessed Callistus, pope and martyr. By order of the emperor Alexander, after being a long time kept in prison without food, and daily scourged with rods, he was finally hurled from the window of the house in which he had been shut up, and cast into a well, and thus merited the triumph awarded to conquerors.

The Fifteenth of October.

At Avila, in Spain, St. Teresa, virgin, mother and mistress of the Carmelite Brothers and Sisters of the Strict Observance ✝ *Among those with the reputation of sanctity, at Perryville, Missouri, the Venerable Servant of God, Father Felix DeAndreis, C.M., Vicar General of the Diocese of Louisiana, and first Superior of the Congregation of the Mission in the United States. Born in Italy, December 13, 1778, he entered the Congregation of the Mission (Lazarists) at Mondovi. He was constantly engaged in giving missions and retreats for the clergy or the seminarists. Pius VII appointed him for the missions of Bishop Dubourg in Louisiana; he directed the novitiate of the Congregation in the Bishop's residence at St. Louis, where he died. His zeal and strenuous life as well as the hardships of missionary work in America had exhausted his weak constitution. His process of beatification has been begun by the Roman authorities.*

The Sixteenth of October.

The feast of St. Hedwig, widow, duchess of Poland, who went to her rest in the Lord on the 15th of this month. — In many churches, the feast of St. Margaret Alacoque, whose feast was transferred to this day by Pope Paul VI. Her birthday is on the day following.

The Seventeenth of October.

At Paray, in France, the birthday of St. Margaret Mary Alacoque. She made her profession in the Order of the Visitation of Blessed Mary the Virgin, and she achieved great merit in spreading public devotion to the Most Sacred Heart of Jesus. Pope Benedict XV added her to the calendar of the saints. — In many churches, the memory of St. Ignatius of Antioch. He was for many centuries honored on the 1st of February, transferred to this day by Pope Paul VI.

The Eighteenth of October.

The birthday of blessed Luke, evangelist, who, after having suffered much for the name of Christ, died in Bithynia, filled with the Holy Ghost. — At Ossernenon, near Auriesville, New York, the birthday of St. Isaac Jogues and St. Jean de Lalande,

St. Isaac Jogues

martyrs. From Quebec Jogues went to the regions around the great lakes where the illustrious Father Brebeuf and others were laboring. Near Three Rivers he was taken prisoner by the Iroquois and, after being cruelly tortured, carried to the Indian village of Ossernenon (Auriesville) on the Mohawk, about 40 miles above the present city of Albany. When, after 13 months of slavery, he was about to be burnt at the stake, he was freed by the Dutch and conveyed to France. There he was received with great honors at court. He returned to Canada and negotiated peace with the Indians at Ossernenon, then began his third and last journey to the Mohawk, who ascribed to him the double calamity of a contagious fever and of a blight which had fallen on their crops. Their warriors met him near Lake George, stripped him naked, slashed him with their knives and then, with a faithful layman, Jean Lalande, led him to the village. When entering a cabin, Jogues was struck with a tomahawk and afterwards decapitated, and the next day Lalande met the same fate. Their heads were fixed on the palisades, the bodies thrown into the Mohawk. Their memory is kept with the other North American martyrs on September 26th or on October 19th.

The Nineteenth of October.

The memory of the North American Martyrs: Sts. René Goupil, Isaac Jogues, Jean de Lalande,

Jean de Brébeuf, Gabriel Lalemant, Antoine Daniel, and Charles Garnier. Their feast was established on the 26th of September by Pope Pius XI, who raised them to the altars, and it was then transferred to this day by Pope Paul VI. — At Arenas, in Spain, St. Peter of Alcantara, confessor, of the Order of Minorites, who was canonized by Clement IX on account of his admirable penance and many miracles.

The Twentieth of October.

In some churches, the memory of St. John Cantius, priest and confessor. Being glorious for virtues and miracles, he was inscribed among the saints by the Sovereign Pontiff, Clement XIII. — In many churches, the memory of St. Paul of the Cross, honored on this day since the time of Paul VI.

The Twenty-first of October.

In Cyprus, the holy abbot Hilarion. His life, full of virtues and miracles, was written by St. Jerome.—At Cologne, Germany, the birthday of the Saints Ursula and her companions, who gained the martyrs' crown by being massacred by the huns for the Christian religion and their constancy in keeping their virginity. Many of their bodies were deposited at Cologne.

The Twenty-second of October.

At Rome, the memory of Pope Saint John Paul II, renowned for his holiness of life and his travels around the world. His birthday is on the 2nd of April.

The Twenty-third of October.

At Fontfroide, France, the memory of St. Anthony Mary Claret, bishop and founder of the Missionary Sons of the Immaculate Heart of Mary. He entered heaven on the following day. — The birthday of St. John of Capistrano, who formerly was honored on the 28th of March.

The Twenty-fourth of October.

The feast of the holy archangel St. Raphael, known as the angelical physician of soul and body. — In many churches, the memory of St. Anthony Mary Claret, who was traditionally honored on the previous day.

The Twenty-fifth of October.

At Rome, the holy martyrs Chrysanthus, and his wife, Daria. After many sufferings endured for Christ, under the prefect Celerinus, they were ordered by the emperor Numerian to be thown into a sandpit on the Salarian road, where, being overwhelmed with earth and stones, they were buried alive. ✝ *Among those with the reputation of martyrdom, at Onondaga, New York, Stephen Teganonakoa, Martyr. He was an Iroquois and a native of Onondaga, but, to ensure the liberty of practicing his religion, had, with his family, retired to Caughnawaga, Canada. While hunting, he was surprised by a Cayuga party and conducted to Onondaga. He was forced to run the gauntlet and undergo the usual tortures, defiantly making the sign of the cross with his mutilated hands. He next suffered the torture of fire; and, triumphing over all was at last bound to the stake. Yet all their cruelty could not wring a sigh from the Iroquois hero who stood motionless, his eyes raised to heaven. At last he chanted aloud his dying prayer, a prayer for his torturers, who in a few moments completed their work.*

The Twenty-sixth of October.

At Rome, in the time of the emperor Hadrian, St. Evaristus, pope and martyr, who enriched the Church of God with his blood.

The Twenty-eighth of October.

The birthday of the blessed apostles Simon the Cananean, and Thaddeus, who is called Jude. Simon preached the Gospel in Egypt, Thaddeus in Mesopotamia. Afterwards, entering Persia together, they converted to Christ a numberless multitude of the inhabitants, and then underwent martyrdom.

The Thirty-first of October.

The vigil of All Saints Day, popularly called Halloween.

Presentation of the Virgin

St. Martin of Tours

All Souls

St. Cecilia

St. Andrew

November

The First of November.

THE FESTIVAL OF ALL SAINTS, which pope Boniface IV, after the dedication of the Pantheon, ordained to be kept generally and solemnly every year, in the city of Rome, in honor of the blessed Virgin Mary, Mother of God, and of the holy martyrs. It was afterwards decreed by Gregory IV that this feast, which was then celebrated in many dioceses, but at different times, should be on this day perpetually and solemnly kept by the whole Church in honor of all the saints. ✠ *Among those with the reputation of sanctity, at Rochester, Minnesota, the Servant of God, Archbishop Vincent J. McCauley, C.S.C., missionary and bishop of Fort Portal in Uganda. Permission to proceed with the cause has been given by the Vatican.*

The Second of November.

The Commemoration of all the faithful departed.

The Third of November.

At Lima, Peru, the memory of St. Martin de Porres, religious, servant of the poor and sick, and worker of miracles. He was enrolled among the saints by Pope John XXIII.

The Fourth of November.

At Milan, Italy, St. Charles Borromeo, cardinal and bishop of that city, who was ranked among the saints by Paul V on account of the holiness of his life and his renown for miracles. — At Bologna, Italy, the holy martyrs Vitalis and Agricola. The former was first the servant of the latter, and afterwards his partner and colleague in martyrdom. He was subjected by the persecutors to all kinds of torments, so that there was no part of his body without wounds. After having suffered with constancy, he yielded up his soul to God in prayer. Agricola was put to death by being fastened to a cross with many nails. ✝ *Among those with the reputation of martyrdom, at San Diego, California, Father Luis Jayme, O.F.M. He arrived at San Diego, with nine other Fathers. The Fathers had been fairly successful in their efforts to win the Indians from paganism; this provoked the sorcerers and other chief men to conspire against their lives. During the night, about one thousand armed Diegueño Indians surrounded the mission, looted the sacristy and storehouse and then set fire to the buildings. Father Luis Jayme and Jose Romero, the blacksmith, were killed. Father Luis was the first martyr of the California mission. — Among those with the reputation of sanctity, at Sacramento, California the birthday of the Servant of God Alphonse Gallegos, O.A.R., auxiliary bishop of Sacramento who was known as the "bishop of the barrio". His cause was approved by Pope Benedict XVI.*

The Fifth of November.

In some places, the Feast of the Holy Relics. ✝ *Among those with the reputation of martyrdom, at Nacagdoches, Texas, the Franciscan Father Antonio Diaz de Leon. He was from the Franciscan College of Zacatecas, Mexico, known for his virtues and merits and had been on the mission at San Jose and acted as chaplain to the troops. For ten years he was at Nacagdoches mission when turbulent American frontiersmen and their itinerant ministers began to stir up animosity against the Church. He was shot under mysterious circumstances while kneeling.*

The Sixth of November.

Among those with the reputation of martyrdom, at Barcelona and Moncada, Spain, Blessed Father Lucas Tristany, OCD and Blessed Father Eduardo Farré, OCD and companions. They served at various parishes in the Diocese of Tuscon, Arizona and became American citizens, but eventually returned to Spain. When the Civil War broke out, Father Lucas was superior of a Carmelite monastery that was burned down by a Leftist mob, and he was beaten with rifle butts and then shot in the back. Father Eduardo, then prior of the community at Tarragona, was seized from a private home at gunpoint on July 25 and never heard from again. Fathers Lucas and Eduardo were beatified in a group of 498 martyrs of the Spanish Civil War by Pope Benedict XVI. — Among those with the reputation of sanctity, at La Prairie, Canada, Catherine Gandeaktenha. A girl of the Erie nation when it was destroyed by the Iroquois, she was carried off a slave to the Oneidas. She married a baptized Huron and was instructed in the faith by Father Jacques Bruyas as she taught him the language. Baptized by Bishop Laval at Quebec, she then settled with her husband at La Prairie de la Magdelaine, where she became renowned for her sweetness and charity towards all who passed that way. Her cabin soon attracted other Christian Iroquois, creating the mission of St. Francis Xavier. She was the foremost in devotion at the mission and introduced the Holy Family Confraternity there. She died after an illness and was interred at La Prairie, her remains claimed by both the Indians and the French.

The Eighth of November.

On the Lavican way, the birthday of the saintly brothers, Severus, Severian, Carpophorus and Victorinus, called the Four Holy Crowned Martyrs, who were scourged to death with leaded whips, during the reign of Diocletian.

The Ninth of November.

At Rome, the dedication of the Basilica of our Savior. — At Amasea, in Pontus, the birthday of St. Theodore, a soldier, in the time of the emperor Maximian. For the confession of Christ, he was severely scourged and sent to prison, where he was comforted by an apparition of our Lord, who exhorted him to act with courage and constancy. He was finally stretched on the rack, lacrated with iron hooks till his intestines were laid bare, and then cast into the flames to be burned alive.

The Tenth of November.

At Naples, in Italy, the birthday of St. Andrew Avellino, Clerk Regular, very celebrated for his sanctity, and his zeal in procuring the salvation of souls. Being renowned for miracles, he was inscribed in the catalog of saints by Clement XI. — The birthday of the holy martyrs Tryphon and Respicius, and the virgin Nympha. — At Rome, the birthday of St. Leo the Great, pope and confessor. He is honored in many churches on this day, his feast transferred from the 11th of April by Pope Paul VI.

The Eleventh of November.

At Tours, in France, the birthday of St. Martin, bishop and confessor, whose life was so renowned for miracles that he received the power to raise three persons from the dead. — At Cotyæum, in Phrygia, during the persecution of Diocletian, the celebrated martyrdom of St. Mennas, Egyptian soldier, who cast off the military belt and obtained the grace of serving the King of heaven secretly in the desert. Afterwards coming out publicly, and freely declaring himself a Christian, he was first subjected to dire torments; and finally kneeling in prayer, and giving thanks to our Lord Jesus Christ, he was struck with the sword. After his death, he was renowned with many miracles.

The Twelfth of November.

The feast of St. Martin, pope and martyr. Because he had convoked a council at Rome, and condemned the heretics Sergius, Paul and Pyrrhus, he was taken prisoner treacherously by order of the heretical emperor Constans, carried to Constantinople and banished to Chersonesus, Ukraine, where he ended his life, consumed with afflictions endured for the Catholic faith, and with a reputation for many miracles.

The Thirteenth of November.

At Chicago, Illinois, the memory of St. Frances Xavier Cabrini, M.S.C. Attracted by the religious life, she asked to join the Daughters of the Sacred Heart but was rebuffed for reasons of poor health. Instead she began to teach and operated a girls' orphanage with five other women. They took vows in 1877 and founded a new institute, the Missionaries of the Sacred Heart of Jesus. She intended to go to the Chinese missions, but in an audience with Pope Leo XIII he advised "Not to the East, but to the West." Her community arrived in New York and started an orphanage, the first of many institutions including other orphanages, hospitals, and private and parish schools across the United States. She was enrolled in the catalog of the saints by Pope Pius XII. —

St. Frances Xavier Cabrini

At Alcalá de Henares in Spain, St. Didacus, confessor, of the Order of Minorites, whose birthday occurred on the twelfth of this month. — At Vitebsk, in Belarus, the birthday of St. Josaphat, bishop and martyr. He is honored on this day by many churches, and by others on the 14th of November. ✝ *Among those with the reputation of sanctity, at Nawabganj, Bangladesh, the Servant of God Father William P. Evans C.S.C., missionary. During Bangladesh's War for Independence, he was bayoneted and shot by soldiers from Pakistan.*

The Fourteenth of November.

In some churches, the festival of St. Josaphat, bishop and martyr, which was transferred to the 12th of this month by Pope Paul VI.

The Fifteenth of November.

At Cologne, Germany, St. Albert the Great, bishop, confessor, and doctor of the Church.

The Sixteenth of November.

In Germany, St. Gertrude, virgin, of the Order of St. Benedict, who was renowned for the revelations she received. — At Edinburgh, in Scotland, the birthday of St. Margaret, queen, who was renowned for her love of the poor and voluntary poverty. Many churches honor her on this day, others on the 10th of June.

The Seventeenth of November.

In some places, the festival of St. Rose Philippine Duschesne, whose birthday is the following day. — At Neocæsarea, in Pontus, the birthday of St. Gregory, bishop, illustrious by his learning and sanctity. The prodigies and miracles which he wrought to the great glory of the Church gained for him the surname of Wonder-worker. — At Marburg, in Germany, the demise of St. Elizabeth, widow, daughter of Andrew, king of Hungary, of the Third Order of St. Francis. After a life passed in the performance of pious works, she went to heaven, having a reputation for miracles.

✛ *Among those with the reputation of sanctity, at New Orleans, Louisiana, the Venerable Mother Henriette Delille, S.S.F., foundress. As a Creole expected to enter in the concubinage then typical of New Orleans society, she instead consecrated herself to God. With other Creole women she devoted her life to caring for the elderly and infirm as well as to educating slaves and the poor, formally organizing as the Sisters of the Holy Family. Pope Benedict XVI declared her virtues heroic.*

The Eighteenth of November.

At St. Charles, Missouri, the memory of Saint Rose Philippine Duchesne, Virgin, foundress, in America, of the first houses of the Society of the Sacred Heart. Born at Grenoble, France, she set out with four companions for the missions of America.

St. Rose Philippine Duchesne

Bishop Dubourg welcomed her to New Orleans, whence she sailed up the Mississippi to St. Louis, finally settling her little community at St. Charles. Cold, hunger and illness, opposition, ingratitude and calumny served only to fire her lofty and indomitable spirit with new zeal. Having founded the new houses at Florissant, Grand Coteau, New Orleans, St. Louis and St. Michel, La., she yearned to teach poor Indians. Old and broken as she was, she went to labor amongst the Pottowatomies at Sugar Creek, Kansas. But one year later she returned to St. Charles and died. She was raised to the altars by Pope John Paul II. — At Rome, the Dedication of the basilicas of the holy apostles Peter and Paul. The former, having been enlarged, was on this day solemnly consecrated by Urban VIII, while the latter, more sumptuously rebuilt after its total destruction by the flames, was solemnly dedicated on the 10th of December by Pius IX, though the festival in commemoration of that event was transferred to this day.

The Nineteenth of November.

In some churches, the feast of St. Elizabeth of Hungary, widow. She is honored by many others on her birthday, on the 17th of this month. — The memory of St. Pontian, pope and martyr. His feast was formerly celebrated on this day, and was transferred to the 13th of August by Pope Paul VI.

The Twentieth of November.

St. Felix of Valois, priest, confessor, and cofounder of the Order of the Most Holy Trinity for the Redemption of Captives. — In East Anglia, in England, the birthday of St. Edmund, king and martyr.

The Twenty-first of November.

In the temple at Jerusalem, the Presentation of the Blessed Virgin Mary, Mother of God.

The Twenty-second of November.

At Rome, St. Cecilia, virgin and martyr, who brought to the faith of Christ her spouse Valerian and his brother Tiburtius, and encouraged them to martyrdom. After their death, being arrested by the order of Almachius, prefect of the city, and exposed to the fire, from which she came out uninjured, she terminated her glorious sufferings by the sword, in the time of the emperor Marcus Aurelius Severus Alexander. ✝ *Among those with the reputation of sanctity, at Santa Clara, California, the venerable Servant of God, the Franciscan missionary Magin Catalá, O.F.M. He was sent to the Indian mission of Santa Clara in California, where, in company with Father Jose Viader, he labored most zealously for 36 years. All through his life*

Father Catala suffered intensely from inflammatory rheumatism; in his last years he could neither walk nor stand unassisted. He, nevertheless, visited the sick and preached in Indian and Spanish while seated in a chair at the altar rail. Despite his infirmities he observed the rule strictly, used the discipline and penitential girdle and never used meat, fish, eggs or wine. The venerable missionary was famed far and wide for his miracles and prophecies, as well as for his virtues. He died at Santa Clara, and Archbishop Alemany instituted the process of his beatification.

The Twenty-third of November.

The birthday of pope St. Clement, who held the sovereign Pontificate the third after the blessed apostle Peter. In the persecution of Trajan, he was banished to Chersonesus where, being precipitated into the sea with an anchor tied to his neck, he was crowned with martyrdom. — At Rome, St. Felicitas, mother of seven sons, martyrs. After them she was beheaded for Christ, by order of the emperor Marcus Antoninus. — The memory of St. Columban, abbot, who founded many convents and governed a large number of monks. He died at an advanced age, celebrated for many virtues. — At Mexico City, in Mexico, the birthday of Blessed Miguel Pro, priest and martyr. Under the persecution of President Calles he was condemned without trial and shot by firing squad as he raised his arms in the form of a cross.

The Twenty-fourth of November.

In some churches, the feast of St. John of the Cross, priest and doctor of the Church. His birthday is on the 14th of December. — The same day, the birthday of St. Chrysogonus, martyr. After a long imprisonment in chains for the constant confession of Christ, he was by order of Diocletian taken to Aquileia, where he terminated his martyrdom by being beheaded and thrown into the sea. — The memory of the martyrs of Vietnam, St. Andrew Dung-Lac and companions, who earned their crowns at various times and places. They were enrolled in the catalog of the saints by Pope John Paul II.

The Twenty-fifth of November.

The birthday of St. Catharine, virgin and martyr, under the emperor Maximinus. For the confession of the Christian faith, she was cast into prison at Alexandria, and afterwards endured a long scourging with whips garnished with metal, and finally ended her martyrdom by decapitation.

The Twenty-sixth of November.

At Fabriano, Italy, St. Sylvester, abbot, founder of the Congregation of the Sylvestrine monks. — At Alexandria, the birthday of St. Peter, bishop of that city, adorned with all virtues, who was beheaded by the command of Galerius Maximian. + *Among those with the reputation of martyrdom, at Pecos, Texas, Father Juan de la Cruz, O.F.M. With Brother Luis de Ubeda he had accompanied Father Juan de Padilla, when Coronado went to the Northwest to find the legendary Seven Cities of Cibola. Coronado returned to Mexico but the Franciscans remained with the Indians. After having labored for some time amongst the Tiguex on the Rio Grande, Padilla went to Quivira in the Northeast. Father Juan de la Cruz remained to instruct the Tiguex and gave up his life among them.*

The Twenty-seventh of November.

The feast of Our Lady of the Miraculous Medal.

The Twenty-eighth of November.

At Enghien-les-Bains, France, St. Catherine Labouré, religious. Favored by visions of the Blessed Virgin, she propagated the Miraculous Medal and its devotion. + *Among those with the reputation of martyrdom, at Natchez, Mississippi, Father Paul Du Poisson S.J. He was one of the French missionaries who came to the mission in*

Louisiana. He reached the Arkansas Post, which mission had seen no priest since the death of Father Foucault. Here du Poisson labored amongst the Quapaws and the colonists with indifferent success. About that time the Natchez had planned a revolt against the French. On his way to New Orleans Father Du Poisson, ignorant of the plot, reached Natchez and officiated for the people on the first Sunday in Advent. Whilst he was about to carry the Blessed Sacrament to a sick man, he was killed by the Natchez chief with a blow of the tomahawk, after which the chief hacked off his head.

The Twenty-ninth of November.

At Toulouse, in the time of Decius, the holy bishop Saturninus, who was confined by the pagans to the capitol of that city, and from the highest part of the building precipitated down the stairs, by which fall, having his head crushed, his brains dashed out and his whole body mangled, he rendered his worthy soul to our Lord. ✝ *Among those with the reputation of sanctity, at New York, New York, the birthday of the Servant of God Dorothy Day, foundress of the Catholic Worker Movement.*

The Thirtieth of November.

At Patras, in Achaia, the birthday of the apostle St. Andrew, who preached the gospel of Christ in Thrace and Scythia. Being apprehended by the proconsul Ægaeas, he was shut up in prison, severely scourged, and finally, being suspended on a cross, he lived two days on it, teaching the people. Having besought our Lord not to permit that he should be taken down from the cross, he was surrounded with a great brightness from heaven, and when the light disappeared, he breathed his last.

Immaculate Conception

St. John

Nativity

St. Nicholas

St. Lucy

December

The Second of December.

At Rome, the martyrdom of the saintly virgin Bibiana, under the sacrilegious emperor Julian. For the sake of our Lord, she was scourged with leaded whips until she expired.

The Third of December.

On Shangchuan, a Chinese island, St. Francis Xavier, of the Society of Jesus, renowned for the conversions he made among the Gentiles, and for supernatural gifts and miracles. Pius X selected and appointed this holy man to be the heavenly patron of the Society for the Propagation of the Faith and its work.

The Fourth of December.

At Jerusalem, the birthday of St. John Damascene, renowned for sanctity and learning who, by both the written and the spoken word, courageously resisted Leo the Isaurian, in defending the worship paid to sacred images. By order of this emperor his right hand was cut off, but commending himself to an image of the blessed Virgin Mary, which he had defended, his hand was immediately restored to him entire and sound. He was born to eternal life on the 6th of May. — In some places, the feast of St. Peter Chrysologus, bishop of Ravenna, celebrated for his learning and sanctity. His birthday is on the 30th of July. — At Nicomedia, Turkey, the passion of St. Barbara, virgin and martyr, in the persecution of Maximinus. After a series of sufferings, a long imprisonment, burning with torches and the cutting off of her breasts, she terminated her martyrdom by the sword.

The Fifth of December.

In Cappadocia, Turkey, St. Sabbas, abbot, who was renowned in Palestine for admirable examples of sanctity. He labored courageously in defending the Catholic faith against those who attacked the holy council of Chalcedon.

The Sixth of December.

At Myra, Turkey, the birthday of St. Nicholas, bishop and confessor, of whom it is related, among other miracles, that while a great distance from the emperor Constantine, he appeared to him in a vision and moved him to mercy so as to deter him from putting to death some persons who had implored his assistance. ✝ *Among those with the reputation of sanctity, at*

*New York, New York, the Servant of God Fernando Rielo, founder
of the Idente Missionaries of Christ the Redeemer.*

The Seventh of December.

At Milan, the consecration of St. Ambrose, bishop
and doctor of the Church, who has ennobled the
universal Church by his holiness and teaching. — At
the mission of St. Jean, in Ontario, the birthday of
St. Charles Garnier, priest and martyr. During the
Iroquois invasion of Huronia, he refused to leave
his flock and was wounded by musket shots and then
tomahawked outside his chapel. He is honored in the
churches with the rest of his companions on the 26th
of September or the 19th of October. ✝ *Among those
with the reputation of martyrdom, at St. Mark's Island, Florida,
the memory of three unknown Franciscan Fathers. When Governor
Moore of South Carolina made war on Florida, the Christian Indians
on the islands, from St. Catherine's to Amelia, had withdrawn to
St. Mark's Island, where they formed three towns. These were now
committed to the flames with their churches and convents; three
Franciscan Fathers fell into the hands of the enemy, while their
Indian converts fled to St. Augustine. The Fathers were killed by
the Indians.*

The Eighth of December.

THE FEAST OF THE IMMACULATE CONCEPTION of the glorious and ever Virgin Mary, Mother of God. On this day Pius IX solemnly declared her to have been by a special privilege of God free from the stain of original sin. Under this title, with enthusiastic acclaim and with unanimous approval and consent, she was declared patroness of the United States of America by the Fathers of the Sixth Provincial Council of Baltimore. — At Sainte-Marie among the Hurons, in Ontario, the birthday of St. Noël Chabanel, priest and martyr, who was slain by an apostate Huron out of hatred of the faith. His memory is kept along with his companions on the 26th of September and the 19th of October. ✝ *Among those with the reputation of sanctity, at New York, New York, the Servant of God, Father Walter Ciszek, S.J., missionary to the Soviet Union who was imprisoned and sent to the Gulag. A diocesan inquiry has been begun for his cause.*

The Ninth of December.

At Mexico City, Mexico, the feast of St. Juan Diego, to whom was granted the apparition of Our Lady of Guadalupe and upon whose tilma was miraculously imprinted the image venerated to this day. ✝ *Among those with the reputation of sanctity, at New York, New York, Venerable Archbishop Fulton J. Sheen. He was born in El Paso, Illinois and was ordained a priest for the Peoria diocese.*

St. Juan Diego with the image of Our Lady of Guadalupe

He served as a professor of philosophy and became a prolific writer and famed lecturer on radio and television, converting many to the Catholic faith. He served as Auxiliary Bishop of New York, Bishop of Rochester, and titular Archbishop of Newport, Wales. Pope Benedict XVI declared his virtues heroic.

The Tenth of December.

At Rome, pope St. Melchiades, who, having suffered much in the persecution of Maximian, rested in the Lord when peace was given to the Church.

The Eleventh of December.

At Rome, St. Damasus, pope and confessor, who condemned the heresiarch Apollinaris, and restored to his see Peter, bishop of Alexandria, who had been driven from it. He also discovered the bodies of many holy martyrs, and wrote verses in their honor. ✝ *Among those with the reputation of martyrdom, near Vicksburg, Mississippi, Father Jean Souel, S.J. He had come from France with Fathers Du Poisson, Dumas and De Guyenne to the Louisiana mission, and he was assigned to the Yazoos, though prostrated by disease. Although his constitution was completely shattered, he took up his residence at the Indian village and devoted himself to the study of the language. The Yazoos were drawn into the conspiracy of the Natchez, and on December 11th killed Father Souel by a volley of musket balls. His faithful slave, who attempted to resist the violence of the murderers, was cut to pieces. The next day they attacked the French fort and massacred all the inmates.*

The Twelfth of December.

The feast of Our Lady of Guadalupe, honoring her apparition and the bestowing of her miraculous image upon the tilma of Saint Juan Diego at Tepeyac Hill, Mexico City. She was proclaimed Patroness of the Americas by Pope John Paul II.

The Thirteenth of December.

At Syracuse, in Sicily, the birthday of St. Lucy, virgin and martyr, in the persecution of Diocletian. By the order of the ex-consul Paschasius, she was delivered to profligates, that her chastity might be insulted, but when they attempted to lead her away, they could not succeed, either with ropes or with many yoke of oxen. Then pouring hot pitch, rosin, and boiling oil over her body without injuring her, they finally plunged a sword into her throat, and thus completed her martyrdom.

The Fourteenth of December.

At Ubeda, in Spain, the birthday of St. John of the Cross, confessor, companion of St. Teresa in reforming the Carmelites. He was formerly honored on the 24th of November, but now by many on this day.

The Sixteenth of December.

At Vercelli, Italy, St. Eusebius, bishop and martyr, who for the confession of the Catholic faith, was banished to Scythopolis and thence to Cappadocia by the emperor Constantius. Afterwards returning to his church, he suffered martyrdom in the persecution of the Arians. His birthday is on the 1st of August. ✝ *Among those with the reputation of sanctity, at Clyde, Missouri, the Servant of God Father Lukas Etlin, O.S.B., chaplain to the Benedictine Sisters and zealous promoter of the Eucharist.*

The Twenty-first of December.

At Myalapore, India, the birthday of the blessed apostle Thomas, who preached the Gospel to the Parthians, the Medes, the Persians and Hyrcanians. Having finally penetrated into India, and instructed those nations in the Christian religion, he died transfixed with lances by order of the king. His remains were first taken to the city of Edessa and then to Ortona. — At Fribourg, Switzerland, the birthday of St. Peter Canisius, priest of the Society of Jesus, confessor and doctor of the Church. He is now honored by many on this day, and by some on the 27th of April, from which his feast was transferred by Pope Paul VI. ✝ *Among those with the reputation of martyrdom, at the pueblo of the Taos Indians in New Mexico, Father Pedro de*

Miranda, O.F.M. He was a native of Avila, Spain, and was killed by the Taos Indians, with two Spanish soldiers, Luis Pacheco and Juan de Estrada.

The Twenty-second of December.

At Chicago, Illinois, the birthday of St. Frances Xavier Cabrini, M.S.C. Her memory was formerly kept on this day, now kept on November 13.

The Twenty-third of December.

In many churches, the memory of St. John Cantius, priest and confessor, whose festival was transferred to this day by Pope Paul VI. He entered heaven on the 24th of December. ✠ *Among those with the reputation of martyrdom, in St. Mark's Mission, near the mouth of Wolf River, Wisconsin, Brother Jean Guerin, S.J. He was the companion, first of Father Menard, then of Father Louis Andre, and he was slain near Oshkosh, Wisconsin, by pagan Outagamies or Fox Indians.*

The Twenty-fourth of December.

The vigil of the Nativity of our Lord Jesus Christ.

The Twenty-fifth of December.

In the seventh day of the creation of the world, when in the beginning God created heaven and earth; three thousand years from the flood; two thousand years from the birth of Abraham; one thousand five hundred years from Moses and the coming of the Israelites out of Egypt; one thousand years from the anointing of King David; in the sixty-fifth week, according to the prophecy of Daniel; in the one hundred and ninety-fourth Olympiad; in the year seven hundred and fifty-two from the founding of the city of Rome; in the forty-second year of the empire of Octavian Augustus, when the whole earth was at peace, in the sixth age of the world, Jesus Christ, eternal God, and Son of the eternal Father, desirous to sanctify the world by His most merciful coming, having been conceived of the Holy Ghost, and nine months having elapsed since his conception, is born in Bethlehem of Juda, having become man of the Virgin Mary. — THE NATIVITY OF OUR LORD JESUS CHRIST, ACCORDING TO THE FLESH.

The Twenty-sixth of December.

At Jerusalem, the birthday of St. Stephen, the first martyr, who was stoned to death by the Jews shortly after the Ascension of our Lord.

The Twenty-seventh of December.

At Ephesus, the birthday of St. John, apostle and evangelist, who, after writing his gospel, and after enduring exile and writing the divine Apocalypse, lived till the time of the emperor Trajan, and founded and governed the churches of all Asia. Worn out with age, he died in the sixty-eighth year after the passion of our Lord, and was buried near Ephesus.

The Twenty-eighth of December.

In Bethlehem, of Juda, the birthday of the Holy Innocents, who were massacred for Christ by king Herod. ✠ *Among those with the reputation of sanctity, at New York, New York, the Servant of God Father Isaac Hecker, C.S.P., evangelist and founder of the Missionary Society of Saint Paul the Apostle or Paulist Fathers. His cause was opened by Cardinal Edward Egan.*

The Twenty-ninth of December.

At Canterbury, in England, the birthday of St. Thomas Becket, bishop and martyr, who for the defense of jusice and ecclesiastical immunities, was struck with the sword in his own basilica by a faction of impious men, and thus went to Christ.

The Thirtieth of December.

Among those with the reputation of sanctity, at Clarkston, Michigan the Servant of God Father John Anthony Hardon, S.J., priest and catechist, theologian, prolific writer, and defender of orthodoxy. His cause has been allowed by the Vatican to proceed.

The Thirty-first of December.

At Rome, the birthday of pope St. Sylvester, who reigned in the time of Constantine the Great, and confirmed the Council of Nicaea. After performing many other holy deeds, he rested in peace.

Appendix A: Local Additions

This General American Martyrology is intended for the entire United States, but it could be further supplemented with entries of importance to specific regions, cities, orders, or communities. By way of example, I have included here a few additional entries for my home diocese of Philadelphia.

The Twenty-Sixth of February

At Old St. Joseph's, Philadelphia, the memory of the dedication of the Church and founding of the Philadelphia mission by Joseph Greaton, 1733.

The Nineteenth of August

At Chesapeake City, Maryland, the memory of Father Joseph Greaton, S.J. He was born in London on the 2d of February, 1679. In 1708 he entered a Jesuit Novitiate and was sent to Maryland around 1720. Oliver calls Father Greaton "the Apostle of Pennsylvania", as he was assigned the state in his missionary circuit and toiled in that State for nearly twenty years before going to the Eastern Shore of Maryland. He founded the parish at Conewago in 1730. He was the founder of Catholicity in Philadelphia; at first his congregation numbered eleven persons. Old St. Joseph's Church, together with the residence in Willing's Alley, was built by Father Greaton in 1733. He died on the 19th of August, 1753.

The Eighth of June

At Philadelphia the memory of Father Felix Joseph Barbelin, S.J., styled "the Apostle of Philadelphia". Born in France, May 30, 1808, he entered the Society of Jesus in 1831 at Whitemarsh, Maryland, and for some years was stationed at Georgetown College as disciplinarian and teacher of French. In 1836 he became assistant pastor of Holy Trinity Church at Georgetown, and in 1838 was transferred to Philadelphia. For more than a quarter of a century he was pastor of Old St. Joseph's, which became, mainly during his term of office, the centre from which radiated Catholic influences throughout the city and diocese. His zeal was untiring. He founded St. Joseph's Hospital and was the first to establish sodalities for men and women and for the young who were always the objects of his fatherly solicitude. In 1852 he was appointed the first President of St. Joseph's College. His many good works brought him into contact with most of the Catholics of the city, while his charity towards all and particularly his love of children and devotion to their interests made him an object of veneration to Catholics and Protestants alike. He died June 8, 1869, his memory held in benediction.

Appendix B: The Necrology

The necrology is an old devotion that is closely associated with the martyrology. As practiced in the monastic communities, it consisted of notations added to the martyrology entries, marking when members of the order died so that they could be remembered and prayed for on the anniversaries of their passing.

This monastic custom can be very easily adapted by the lay faithful for the remembrance of loved ones, by adding notations at the appropriate date in the margins of this book. Necrology entries should always be read last, after the entries for venerables and servants of God, using the following or a similar prayer:

> On the same day, the anniversary of the passing of our [father/mother/friend, *etc.*] N., who was dear to our household. Eternal rest grant unto him [or her, *etc.*] O Lord, and may the perpetual light shine upon him. May he rest in peace, Amen. May his soul and the souls of all the faithful departed, through the mercy of God, rest in peace, Amen.

INDEX

A

St. Abachum	Jan. 19
St. Abdon	Jul. 30
St. Achilleus	May 12
St. Acutius	Sep. 19
St. Adalbert	Apr. 23
St. Adauctus	Aug. 30
St. Adrian of Canterbury	Sep. 19
St. Agapitus	Aug. 18
St. Agapitus, Martyr	Sep. 20
St. Agatha	Feb. 5
St. Agnes	Jan. 21, 28
St. Agricola	Nov. 4
St. Aidan	Aug. 27
St. Alban	Jun. 20
St. Albert the Great	Nov. 15
St. Alexander	May 3
St. Alexander, Martyr	Jul. 10
St. Alexius	Jul. 17
All Hallows Eve	Oct. 31
All Saints	Nov. 1
All Souls	Nov. 2
Alonzo Giraldo Terreros	Mar. 16
St. Aloysius Gonzaga	Jun. 21
Aloysius Schwartz	Mar. 16
Alphonse Gallegos	Nov. 4
St. Alphonsus Ligouri	Aug. 1, 2
Amador Cuipa Feliciano	Jan. 31
St. Anastasius	Jan. 22
St. Ambrose	Dec. 7
Andrés Quintana	Oct. 12
St. Andrew	Nov. 30
St. Andrew Avellino	Nov. 10
St. Andrew Corsini	Feb. 4
St. Andrew Dung-Lac	Nov. 24
St. Andrew Kim Taegon	Sep. 20
Angel Miranda	Jan. 31
St. Angela Merici	Jan. 27, Jun 1
St. Anicestus	Apr. 17
St. Anne	Jul. 26
St. Anne Line	Aug. 30
Annunciation	Mar. 25
St. Anselm	Apr. 21
St. Ansgar	Feb. 3
St. Anthony of Padua	Jun. 13
St. Anthony Maria Zaccaria	Jul. 5
St. Anthony Mary Claret	Oct. 23, 24
St. Anthony the Abbot	Jan. 17
St. Antoine Daniel	Jul. 4, Oct. 19
St. Antoninus	May 10
Antonio Carbonel	Jun. 4
Antonio de Badajoz	Sep. 17
Antonio Diaz de Leon	Nov. 5
Antonio Enija	Jan. 31
Antonio Margil	Aug. 6
Antonio Mora	Aug. 11
Antonio Moreno	Jun. 8
Antonio Sanchez de Pró	Aug. 11
St. Apollinaris	Jul. 20, 23
St. Apollonia	Feb. 9
Assumption	Aug. 15
St. Athanasius	May 2
St. Audifax	Jan. 19
Augustin a S. Maria	Aug. 31
Augustin Rodriquez (Ruiz)	May 20
St. Augustine of Hippo	Aug. 28
St. Augustine of Canterbury	May 27, 28
St. Augustine Zhao Rong	Jul. 9
Augustus Tolton	Jul. 9

B

St. Barbara	Dec. 4
St. Barnabas	Jun. 11
St. Bartholomew	Aug. 24
St. Basil the Great	Jan. 2, Jun. 14
St. Basilides	Jun. 12
St. Bede	May 25, 27
St. Benedict of Nursia	Mar. 21, Jul. 11
St. Benedict Biscop	Jan. 12
St. Bernard of Clairvaux	Aug. 20
Bernard J. Quinn	Apr. 9
St. Bernardine of Siena	May 20
Bias Rodriguez	Sep. 16
St. Bibiana	Dec. 1
St. Blaise	Feb. 3
St. Bonaventure	Jul. 14, 15
St. Boniface	Jun. 5
St. Boniface, Martyr	May 14
St. Bridgit	Jul. 23, Oct. 8
St. Bruno	Oct. 6

C

St. Caius	Apr. 22
St. Cajetan	Aug. 7
St. Callistus	Oct. 14

D

E

I

J

The Christian Roman Empire (CRE) series
available from Arx Publishing

The Complete Works of Saint Cyprian
    edited by Phillip Campbell

The Life of the Blessed Emperor Constantine: In Four Books
from 306 to 337 AD
    by Eusebius Pamphilus

The Life of Saint Augustine: A Translation of the Sancti Augustini Vita
by Possidius, Bishop of Calama
    by Herbert T. Weiskotten

The Life of Saint Simeon Stylites: A Translation of the Syriac in Bedjan's
Acta Martyrum et Sanctorum
    by Rev. Frederick Lent

The Ecclesiastical History of Evagrius: A History of the Church
from AD 431 to AD 594
    by Edward Walford

The Book of the Popes (Liber Pontificalis): To the Pontificate of Gregory I
    Translated by Louise Ropes Loomis

The Dialogues of Saint Gregory the Great
    edited by Edmund G. Gardner

For more information on this series, see our website at:
www.evolpub.com/CRE/CREseries.html

The Fontes Mediaevalium (FM) series
available from Arx Publishing

The First Crusade: Accounts of Eye-Witnesses and Participants
    edited by August Krey

The Life of Saint Hugh of Avalon: Bishop of Lincoln 1186–1200
    by Gerald of Wales, edited and translated by Richard M. Loomis

For more information on this series, see our website at:
www.evolpub.com/FM/FMseries.html

www.ingramcontent.com/pod-product-compliance
Lightning Source LLC
Chambersburg PA
CBHW022017090426
42739CB00006BA/180